AMERICA
Ailing from the Plague of Male Dominance!

Why & How Males Have Degraded the Country!

DEDICATION

This book is dedicated to females, virtually all of whom have been oppressed, abused and otherwise mistreated by males since the origin of the human species—and most of whom still today are treated like a lower order of human beings who do not have the same intellectual and spiritual capacity of males and continue to be denied the rights and privileges of males by male-created political systems, economic systems, religions and societies in general.
This failure of humanity can
only be redressed by
a female rebellion

THE FAILURE OF MALE DOMINANCE

AMERICA
Ailing from the Plague of Male Dominance!

Why & How Males Have Degraded the Country!

Boyé Lafayette De Mente

A PHOENIX BOOKS ORIGINAL

Other Books by the Author

THE FAILURE OF MALE DOMINANCE

THE FAILURE OF MALE DOMINANCE

Samurai Principles & Practices that will Help Preteens & Teens
in School, Sports, Social Activities
& Choosing Careers
Romantic Hawaii—Sun, Sand, Surf & Sex
Women of the Orient
Asian Face Reading—Unlock the Secrets
Hidden in the Human Face
Why Ignorance, Stupidity and Violence Plague Mankind
Bridging Cultural Barriers in China, Japan, Korea & Mexico
Brave New World of American Sex!
ONCE A FOOL—From Japan to Alaska by
Amphibious Jeep

[Books on Arizona]
Amazing Arizona—Fascinating Facts, Legends & Tall Tales
Visitor's Guide to Arizona's Indian Reservations
The Grand Canyon Answer Book—Everything You Might
Want to Know and Then Some!
America's Famous Hopi Indians—Their Spiritual
Way of Live & Incredible Prophecies!
Arizona's Lords of the Land—The History, Traditional
Customs & Wisdom of the Navajos

***Several of these titles also available in Chinese, Czech,
French, German, Hebrew, Italian, Indonesian, Japanese,
Polish, Portuguese, Russian & Spanish editions.*

CONTENTS

*

The world is a stage
and we are all actors.
Each actor plays a unique part
and is responsible for
his or her own actions.
Responsibility means doing
the right thing no matter
how big or small
the task may be.
Each one of us has a special role to play
in the making the world
a better place.

—*Innerspace*—

[1]

Why Men Created Gods

When the awareness of human beings finally evolved beyond the need for survival, food and sex they began to wonder about life and the world around them—how it all came about.

There was something in the evolving human mind that led them to assume that there must be unseen supernatural spirits or gods who created the human race and the world around them.

This longing for answers was obviously a common trait in the evolution of the human species as virtually all if not all groups of people—no matter how few they were or how isolated they were from each other— came up with a roster of spirit-gods to explain everything in their world—the sun, the weather, other life forms and so on.

Virtually all of these spirit-gods were created by men who gave the principal ones masculine traits, became their exclusive spokesmen and acted as their agents in establishing codes of conduct for their particular societies.

A primary theme in the doctrines established by the main surrogate male gods was the inherent superiority of males over females and the tenet that females were created to serve males. This alone was enough to prevent human beings from achieving their potential, but there were other fundamental elements in the male mindset that were equally damaging to the human species and the cultures that individual human groups created.

Male discrimination against females did not begin as a religious thing. It evolved naturally from the genetic programming of males, so when men created gods the gods naturally consigned women to an inferior status.

Males in virtually all species are genetically designed to be sexually aggressive, to impregnate as many females as possible and to take by force and keep exclusive sexual rights to as many females as possible.

This instinctive behavior in the earliest human males was buttressed by the fact that they recognized that *females are inherently more sexually potent than males.*

Females can engage in sex dozens of times a day whether they really want to or not because they don't have to get a hard-on to do it and are not as exhausted as males are by the sexual climax—if they have one.

Males on the other hand, more often than not, achieve sexual climaxes in a matter of minutes because in earlier times engaging in sex left them susceptible to attack by competing males so they had to do it quickly.

Furthermore, most males, including younger ones, cannot repeat the sex act more than two or three times in rapid succession and still enjoy it. It not only loses its power to pleasure, it becomes painful.

And it was this sexual reality that resulted in early males doing everything in their power—physically, emotionally, intellectually and spiritually—to control women; to make them subservient not only sexually but in all other aspects of life.

While some primate species, like monkeys, can perform sexually several times a day day-after-day, even the most potent human male is satiated after three or four times at most. When a human male achieves a sexual climax it releases the sexual energy that has built up over a period of time, and it takes time for this energy to rebuild.

By the time the average male is in his late 30s this buildup of sexual energy generally requires two or three if not more days, during which his interest in sex is emotional instead of a physical need.

The hype that manufacturers use to sell drugs like Viagra—which artificially create erections of the male organ for an hour or more with the promise that men can have sexual intercourse several times a day day-after-day if so desired—is both misleading and dangerous.

The billion-dollar-a-year success of Viagra naturally inspired copycats—the hype of one of them, called Aspire 36 Plus, described as a fast-acting liquid, says that in addition to improving arousal it "enhances the entire experience from beginning to toe-curling end giving you both uninhibited satisfaction yet you'll still be ready for round two, three or four!!!" The ads go on to say that it keeps on working, again and again, "reducing recovery time for an encore performance!"

Males who have a hard-on for more than an hour or so without having a climax quickly discover that it is extremely uncomfortable and sometimes very painful if the sexual stimulation from kissing or other activity that doesn't result in a climax is intense and prolonged. Teenage boys who neck with girls for long periods without going all the way find this out soon enough.

Having a hard-on for several hours—as some of the sex drug makers admit—becomes a medical problem that requires the intervention of a doctor who can administer [as you would expect!] another drug to counteract the sex drug.

In other words, it is not natural or actually possible for human males to become as sexually potent as females because nature was not and still is not that equitable. The make-up of male and female sexuality was designed to ensure that life goes on despite all of the dangers it presented—not to make males and females sexual equals.

Subsequent religious taboos, customs and laws designed to control and limit the sexual behavior of both males and females were to have incredible unintentional results.

Generally, the only people who were exempt from these restrictions—or simply chose to ignore them—were the men in charge. Both lay and religious leaders have historically broken the laws they enacted and required common people to obey.

The cultural problems afflicting the present-day world at large are therefore not simple or isolated. Their partial or complete failures include all of the organizations that are associated with civilization—economic, educational, political, and social.

There are still some shining lights in American and other cultures but broadly speaking the various facets of the cultures are a mishmash of conflicting principles, faulty planning, incompetent execution and a number of cancerous elements that represent a serious threat to humanity and to the Earth.

As British philosopher Aldous Huxley once observed: "At least two thirds of our miseries spring from human stupidity, human malice, and those great motivators and justifiers of malice and stupidity: idealism, dogmatism and proselytizing zeal on behalf of religious or political idols."

Before dealing with male-created gods and the male-made religions they spawned it is necessary to address the sexuality of homo sapiens because sex is one of the three key foundations of human behavior. And unfortunately for humanity, the preprogrammed sexual nature of males has played the key role in all cultures created since the appearance of human beings.

[2]

The Misunderstanding & Misuse of Male Sexuality!

What nature obviously did not foresee or plan for was the possibility that male members of the human species would not always have ready access to females for sexual purposes. Males were designed with their gonads always in the "on" position, producing semen and sexual energy 24 hours a day.

The problem with this is that when males are prevented—for whatever reason—from expelling all of the sexual energy that builds up in their gonads and prostate glands the pressure from the unused energy builds up and up, and fairly early in the process begins to affect how males think and act.

One of the most unheralded results of this sexual energy buildup is the relationship between violence and unused male sexual energy. Studies by professionals have shown that the more sexual energy that builds up in males the more likely they are to engage in behavior that includes every form of violence known.

This behavior ranges from verbal and physical abuse of children, girl friends and wives to fighting among themselves, single and mass murders, and wars in which hundreds to millions are maimed and killed.

Just one aspect of the misunderstanding and misuse of human sexuality in ancient as well as modern times is the incarceration of huge numbers of men in prisons where they do not have access to normal sexual release with females. There are also prisons for females who have no access to male sexual partners but their numbers are miniscule compared to males.

In many countries, including the U.S., religious taboos have traditionally prevented prison inmates from having access to partners of the opposite sex. But there are some exceptions.

Mexico, often touted as a strict Catholic country, allows many of its prison inmates to have conjugal visits from wives and girl friends, particularly those who can afford to pay their jailors a fee for the privilege.

This situation exists in Mexico because like other typical Hispanic-influenced Catholic countries most of the men pay no attention to the dictates of the Church [except perhaps on Sundays and special holidays]—

looking at religious beliefs and real life as separate worlds. There is even a special term for this division of real life and religious life in the Catholic Philippines.

The Incredible Masturbation Taboos

The role of the Christian Church in attempting to control the sexual behavior of males has included taboos against masturbation. Until recent times the Church taught that achieving sexual release through masturbation was a sin against God. There is scripture in the Bible that says it is better for males to leave their seed in the bellies of whores than cast it to the wind.

And until modern times some preachers and priests advised mothers of young boys to tie their hands behind their backs at night so they couldn't masturbate while in bed. [It is normal for males to get hard-on's from four to a dozen times every 24 hours, including while asleep, which often wakes them up as they get older.]

As late as the 19th century some Christian mothers were still telling their young sons that masturbating would make them go insane—and still today young males who masturbate do it furtively in order not to be caught and shamed by their parents or other adults. Masturbating by girls has been even more taboo.

Thanks to the religious position on masturbation, the female need and urge to masturbate has given rise to a large industry that manufactures and sells dildos and other masturbation tools for women.

Healthy males get hard-on's from four to eight or more times every 24-hour period, starting when they are still in the womb and continuing until they are in their 70s, 80s or 90s if they live that long.

In advanced countries today men are living into their 70s and 80s and beyond, and during these long life-spans they are having far more erections per day and night than was normal for males in the past because there is more overt sexual stimulation.

This means the average male gets from 2,000 to 3,000 hard-on's per year, of which less than 10 percent are used. You can image what kind of physical and emotional stress this causes.

In addition to this natural phenomena, by the time boys in the United States and some other countries are in their mid-teens they have advanced to necking with girl friends, during which they typically have full, hard, unrelieved erections for as long as an hour or more. This results in significantly increasing the build-up of stress in their prostate glands and gonads—often to the point that it is extremely painful.

Furthermore, the amount of sexual titillation that present-day males of all ages are exposed to on tele-vision, in magazines, movies, etc., is incredible, and dramatically increases the incidence of regular, daily sexual stress that is not relieved.

If you assume that a male has a partial or complete erection only five times every 24-hour period and lives to be 60 years old that amounts to a total of 109,500 erections. You can assume that these erections were not "used" more than about 100 times a year, for a total of 6,000 during the 60-year period. This leaves males with well over 100,000 unrelieved sexual arou-sals over a period of six decades.

The negative impact this accumulation of stressed-out periods has on the prostate gland has to be horrific—and may be the primary cause of the enlargement of the prostate gland...and may also be associated with the incidence of prostate cancer.

For every year beyond 60 that you add to the life-span of men you have at least an additional 1,800-plus erections—and despite old tales you might have heard, normal, healthy men in their 70s and 80s *do* get hard-on's, and suffer when they are not used.

It's Not a Laughing Matter!

Those who are tempted to laugh this problem off as something that is not really serious would, again, be well advised to consider that unrelieved sexual stress among males is one of the primary sources of all of the male-generated violence that has plagued mankind from the beginning.

The longer normal, healthy males go without releasing the natural buildup of sexual energy the more apt they are to engage in some kind of violence—from abusing their wives and children to taking their frustrations out on other members of society—or engaging in other kinds of destructive behavior.

If you make up a list of all of the cruel, destructive, evil, inhumane, savage and stupid things that have happened to human beings—and are, of course, still happening today—at least ninety-five percent of the people responsible for these things have been and are males.

One of the primary reasons for this male mayhem can be traced to the position taken by the three largest and most powerful religious cults [Judaism, Christianity and Islam], which resulted in males having to repress their natural sexual desires and use up their sexual energy in other ways that were often violent.

The fact that this religious rationale incorporated the concept that females are inferior to males made life even more onerous and destructive for humanity in general.

In simple terms, when a man gets hard on the bottom he gets soft on the top—meaning he cannot think in clear, rational terms and is likely to do irrational things when in a state of sexual arousal.

In the past the only option generally open to young males to expel their sexual energy was masturbation, which was generally effective when early teenage boys were concerned. But masturbation is not the natural solution for adult men. It relieves the physical stress somewhat but not all of the mental/emotional stress—and the relief is short-lived.

Male-dominated religious teachings combined with man-made legal and social sanctions designed to keep women from expending their unused sex energy has caused as much if not more damage to the mental and physical well-being of females.

[3]

The Misunderstanding
& Misuse of
Female Sexuality!

Until recent times virtually all societies ignored the fact that women also have powerful sexual urges and needs—an incredible arrogance perpetrated by males. The emotional and physical suffering this has caused and continues to cause females is incalculable.

Over the millennia the various ailments females suffered from being denied the opportunity to fulfill their sexual needs were invariably linked by males to the overall nature of females—not sexual deprivation. Some men, however, consciously or subconsciously, apparently realized that there was a sexual element in the "disruptive" behavior of females, and their often stated solution was that they needed a "good screw."

However, this insight did not lead to any lessening of the male-created taboos that kept females from being able to use up their sexual energy.

The Role of the Catholic Church

Some of the measures promoted or condoned by the Catholic Church during the so-called Middle Ages to control female sexual behavior are hardly believable today.

Beginning in the 11th century, European church and lay leaders launched a series of religious-inspired military campaigns against Middle East countries in an attempt to free Jerusalem and the other "Holy Cities" from their Moslem occupiers. These so-called "Crusades" against Islamic countries continued off and on for approximately three hundred years.

During this incredibly long period of Pope-backed wars some men had their wives outfitted with "chastity belts"—iron thong-like devices that were locked in place to prevent the women from being able to have sexual intercourse with other males while the husbands were away doing their religious duty.

Many of these lockable iron "chastity belts" were made in Italy, where their manufacture and use was promoted by the Catholic Church. [Even farther out than this device was an older practice among ancient slave holders to have the foreskin of the penises of their adult male slaves sewn tight, leaving only a tiny hole for urination, to discourage them from engaging in sexual intercourse with any woman…another extreme to which men have gone in the past to control sexual behavior.]

Ironically, most of the glory-hungry knights who left Europe in their zeal to take the "Holy Land" away from Moslems never returned home. Some 20 percent of them were killed in battle, and some 60 or 70 percent of them died from the plague and other diseases. History also notes, not surprisingly, that many women managed to get around the iron chastity belts by one means or another, including having a second key made by willing locksmiths.

According to a number of totally unreliable sources on the Internet some form of chastity belts continued to be used in Europe well after the end of the Crusades, and, in fact, into modern times. Such is the terrible hold that religious beliefs have on both men and women.

However, given the male psyche it is not surprising that historically males have gone to inhuman lengths to prevent females from exercising their full sexuality because it is far stronger than that of males.

[4]
Why Women Are Superior to Men!

According to human biology all human beings begin as females, with some of the embryos later developing into males. This is the first sign that "God!" intended for females to be more important than males. In any event, it puts the kibosh on the Adam and Eve fable that God first created a man then took a rib out of the poor fellow and created a woman.

Nature's plan also made sure that females are sexually superior to males. As noted, females can engage in sex dozens of times a day if they want to—or don't want to—while even the most virile male peters out after three or four times at the most and has to wait for hours to days before he is able to produce more semen and sexual energy, get it up and in again, and actually enjoy the act.

And finally, the genetic factor that nails the superiority of the female sex is when women are free to think and behave in a way that is natural for them they are generally more practical, more logical, more rational, and more humane than males—all factors that are essential parts of the make-up of females because they are responsible for the actual creation and nurturing of human life.

In the U.S. and a few other countries the religious concept of female inferiority lost some ground during the 20th century, but even in these countries women are still regarded as and generally treated as inferior to men.

Humanity will continue to be plagued by ignorance, stupidity and violence as long as religious doctrines continue to preach and enforce the superiority of men and the inferiority of women, and prevent women from bringing their innate sense of compassion, cooperation and goodwill to the world at large.

Obviously, the sexual nature of males and the sex-based arrogance that led them to automatically assume that they were superior to females was to have results that went far beyond the oppression of females.

This arrogance and the cultural systems it created continue to plague mankind, and despite the examples of women who have ascended to power in the business and political worlds the underlying faults and failures of the religious-inspired syndrome remain in control in most societies.

The incredible power that Catholicism has traditionally had over the lives of millions of people began to weaken in the mid-1900s, primarily as a result of man-made wars and male-invented technology—the wars forcing males to free women from their homes and farms to work in factories while the men were away fighting and dying; and the new technology, particularly automobiles, making it possible for women to exercise a degree of freedom to go places on their own that they had never had before.

However, the power of the Islamic religion to sub-jugate and oppress Moslem women did not begin to wane significantly until the so-called Arab Spring that started in 2011 when revolutions began in Tunisia, Egypt, Libya and elsewhere against their despotic religious-based governments—but this movement has a long way to go to free females from the shackles of Islam.

[5]

Trials of the Catholic Church

The oppression of females by the Catholic Church began to take a hit with the appearance of *The PILL* in 1960 but it was to be a series of scandals in the late 1900s that finally began to significantly erode the power of the Church over the lives of women.

The 20th Century Sex Scandals

The greatest scandal to hit the Catholic Church at the end of the 20th century was the widespread public disclosure of sexual activity by homosexual and pedophile priests—a practice that had been going on since day one because it was condoned by those in these categories who had risen to high positions in the hierarchy of Church and was also kept quiet by other high-placed members because they didn't want to harm the Church image.

This ongoing situation did not become publicly known nationally or internationally until the advent of news media that was both irreverent and more driven by readership and profit motives. The first reactions of the Catholic Church on the highest level were disingenuous to say the least, but as more and more incidents were revealed and lawsuits mounted, the Church finally admitted the problem and said it would take steps to stop it.

There is also growing lay and some priestly opposition to the Catholic Church doctrine of requiring priests to remain celibate—in part, no doubt, because of the 20th century sex scandals involving priests.

The dogma that abstaining from sexual intercourse with members of the opposite sex results in males and females remaining pure, saintly and god-like, goes back several thousand years. It was not until the 4th century A.D. that it first cropped up in the so-called Western Church. And it was not until the mid-11th century that Pope Gregory VII issued a decree forbiding priests from marrying. [Another reason for this was that when married priests had male children any rights they had to Church-owned land went to the eldest son, diluting the power of the Church—and that had become a serious sore point for the Pope.]

The decree prohibiting priests from marrying or engaged in sex with females was reaffirmed by Popes in the 12th century and again in the 16th century. Despite growing opposition to this ancient practice the decree was again reaffirmed in 2010 by Pope Benedict XVI.

The ancient idea that celibacy contributes to purity in both a physical and divine sense is, of course, absolute nonsense. What it does do is subject the individual to enormous stress that manifests itself in a variety of ways that have long been obvious but have been ignored by the Church hierarchy.

Religions and American Women

American females have also been among those who were deliberately kept ignorant of their own sexual nature as well as that of males until modern times.

In this day and age it is absolutely incredible to admit that just a few generations ago American women were subject to being tied to stakes and burned alive by men who accused them of being witches when they exhibited "unnatural" behavior—generally the result of sex-related frustrations.

It was not until well into the 20th century that a few women began to rebel against the sexual restraints and discrimination females were forced to endure, by writing and speaking and eventually creating a movement that came to be known as "Women's Lib."

The partial success of this movement was a direct out-growth of the new entertainment and news media industries jumping on the Women's Lib bandwagon—not so much because they had become advocates but because of prurient interest in the stories and the fact that they grabbed attention and increased sales profits.

But Women's Lib has made only a small dent in the behavior of males driven by unused sexual energy and a mindset that is still in an ancient self-interest mode based on physical strength, size and an "in-charge" complex that often ignores reality.

Of course, there are millions of civilized and educated men who have risen above this ancient male programming, and their influence is growing but it is far from the point that it can change the course of the institutions that control the bulk of humanity.

As is so obvious it goes without saying that even the most enlightened societies today remain in the grips of ancient patterns of thought and behavior that are patently irrational and destructive not only to human beings but to the Earth and all of its other life forms.

But it also goes without saying that for the first time in human history the knowledge that is necessary to change this doomsday scenario is at hand and the desire for change is growing. The question is when will it really begin to make significant inroads on the power structures that are now in charge.

And the crux of this power structure is bound up in one-god religions—in fact, the biggest tragedy to befall mankind was the creation of the first one-god religion between three and four thousand years ago—a time-frame which reveals clearly that most of its most crucial dogma are false, since the history of mankind is measured in hundreds of thousands of years and that of other life forms in millions of years.

[6]
The One-God Concept

From ancient to virtually modern times all societies had a variety of gods, some numbering in the dozens. While some of the gods had to do with the origin of life, others were the gods of such natural phenomena as the wind, the oceans and mountains.

Jews Create Yahweh/God

Between three and four thousand years ago the religious leaders of the Israelites [Hebrews], a group of Semite tribes who lived in the area of what is now modern Israel, came up with the idea that just one all-powerful god would be far better than many gods, so they decided to worship only one god, whom they referred to as Yahweh. As time passed the Hebrews began to claim that Yahweh was the *only* God and that all who did not believe in and worship him were doomed to go to Hell when they died. Their religion came to be known as Judaism [from the name of one of the Israelite tribes], and its members came to be known as Jews.

The creators of Yahweh [God] knew absolutely nothing about the Earth or world at large, including the many civilizations around the globe and the billions of galaxies and trillions of stars [suns] that make up the universe. So they had no problem in attributing all things in life and nature to their new God, including he belief that creation occurred only a few thousand years earlier—which was as far back as the Jewish people could trace their ancestry.

The Jesus Christ Add-On

Several centuries after the concept of one god became well established in Jewish culture the descendants of the creators of Yahweh took bits and pieces from many other religions—including the concept of virgin birth—and came up with the idea that more people would believe in and worship their God if he sent them a son as his personal go-between, giving birth to the story of Mary and her son who later became known as Jesus Christ the Savior of mankind. [The word "Christ" comes from the Greek term meaning "oil."— with which the Jews bathed the feet of those they regarded as holy.]

The Rise of Christianity

Over the next few hundred years the one-God cult of the Jews morphed into the theological and social cult that came to be known as Christianity, which eventually was split into Catholicism, Protestantism and a mish-mash of other sects, including Mormonism, by males who did not accept all of the teachings of the Catholic Church and had their own ideas of God's will and the proper behavior of men and women.

While the original aim of Christianity—whose founding is often credited to the Jewish tribal leader Abraham—was to assert and maintain human worth and dignity it was soon subverted into a tribal identity and competed with other faiths for social and political power. Thus the numerous wars waged in the name of the Christianity and its offshoots over the millennia and down to modern times.

Still today most Christian sects, especially Catholicism, are basically tribal religions that serve the interests of their male founders and administrators at the expense of females and competing religions.

There is no more stark evidence of the inhumanity of a bigoted god-based religion as the invasion and conquering of the New World in the 1500s by Spanish conquistadors who believed that their Catholic religious beliefs took precedence over the cultures and lives of the millions of people who lived on the Caribbean Islands and the North and South American continents—a phenomenon that was later repeated by English and other European immigrants who began their campaigns to conquer and control—or eradicate—the Native American population in the 1600s.

God's Terrible Swift Sword

In America's Civil War [1861-1865] in which hundreds of thousands of young men were killed and hundreds of thousands of others were horribly mutilated both the North and South sides publicly and loudly proclaimed that God was on their side and that they were doing God's work. Southerners justified their keeping of black human beings as slaves as in keeping with the will of God. Northerners justified their going to war as a fight against evil and sang about "God's terrible swift sword" helping them vanquish the Southern armies.

The military campaigns by the United States government against Native Americans, whom it regarded as pagan savages with few if any rights, did not end until the 1880s. It was not until 1924 that Native Americans, whose ancestors had lived here for thousands of years, were "granted" citizenship by the government that had conspired in killing most of them and depriving the survivors of much or all of their traditional homelands simply because they were different and didn't believe in the Christian God.

What a travesty, and what an indictment against the religious beliefs and practices of early European who invaded and conquered the Americas—an inhuman bias that still exists.

The Power of the God Cult

The power of the cult of Christianity and its offshoots to seduce and hold the minds of the most educated men and women in those ancient times was to shape the future of their followers in ways that could not have been intended—causing, death, destruction and incredible suffering on a massive scale.

Since creation of Yahweh/God the knowledge that human beings have learned about the universe, its origin and how it works, is off the scale, and yet millions of educated people continue to profess belief in the God-concept taught by Judaism, Christianity, Islam and all of their offshoots, and to worship a God who represents all of the elements in the nature of human males, the good and the bad—a form of willful stupidity that is pathological to the extreme.

The only thing more incredible than this ongoing pathological reverence for an imaginary God are the rationales that professed believers in Judaism, Christianity and Islam use to convince themselves and others that there *is* a God who created everything some six thousand year ago and is responsible for everything, despite the obvious evidence to the contrary.

Historically, Jews, Christians and Moslems have slaughtered each other while shouting that God is on their side. When tragic things occur they say it is God's will, while continuing to preach that God is the ultimate guardian and protector of human beings and will save people from evil and disaster if they believe in him and pray to him—or his "son," the young Jew Jesus.

What is now just as incredible is that many people *know* that belief in a benign God creator and protector is absolute nonsense but most of them—especially politicians—are afraid to publicly admit it.

What was weirdly amusing at the turn of the 21st century was that one of the few individuals with a public pulpit who was not afraid to speak the truth about the God fable was a comedian: Bill Maher, the host of *Real Time* on HBO. Bill repeatedly said the God story was all just nonsense.

Promoting and Selling God

Since around 500 A.D. the God fable has become a major industry, and today its various constituents employ several million people. These include managers of institutions like the Catholic Church, Jewish synagogues and Islamic mosques along with a large number of individuals who use the airwaves to con people into sending them money.

Of course, Jewish, Christian and Islamic sects and their hundreds of thousands of churches provide some material support for many of members, but their use of the God fable to attract and hold these members is indefensible.

In addition to perpetrating a false faith these institutions provide people with a way of avoiding personal responsibility for their behavior. The fact that these faiths allow their members to slaughter each other in the name of and for their God is a form of insanity.

The babble of many of the religion-based con men and con women on radio and television is so infantile, so stupid, so obviously put-on, that only people who have been programmed to the moronic level could believe what they say and send them money.

The efforts of obviously well-educated members of the Catholic Church and similar organizations to affirm the existence of a Creator-God are marvelous demonstrations of their skill with words in "proving" something for which there is absolutely no evidence—and incredibly vast amounts of evidence to the contrary.

What is most disturbing and the most dangerous for humanity is that equally well-educated and knowledgeable people in positions of great power and influence cop-out by agreeing with or pretending to agree with the God people.

By this time it should be obvious to all that the most destructive element in God-based moralities is the fact that they are male-oriented and male-dominated.

[7]
The Ongoing Plague of Male Dominance

Virtual and real male dominance over females in virtually every group of human beings that has ever existed has resulted in ignorance, willful stupidity, cruelty and violence plaguing mankind since day one.

As said, male discrimination against females did not begin as a religious thing. It evolved naturally from the genetic programming of males, so when men created gods their gods naturally consigned women to an inferior status.

Because males recognized that females were inherently more sexually potent than they were they did everything in their power—physically, emotionally, intellectually and spiritually—to control women; to make them subservient not only sexually but in all other aspects of life.

But the emergence of civilizations put a kink in the sexual monopoly of big strong males. After the advent of larger organized societies most men, officially at least, had to limit themselves to just one mate at a time, but in most societies many males made sure they still had access to mistresses, concubines, harems and prostitutes.

Judaism, Christianity & Islam

Then in what is now referred to as the Western world—as opposed to Asia—along came Judaism, Christianity and Islam—all of which were created and controlled by men and all of which established "god-given" laws controlling the sexual behavior of men and women, with the laws naturally skewered in favor of men. In these male-created and controlled religions females were an after-thought created to serve men.

As time went by, overly zealous religious leaders and theologians—all males and often men who feared women—began to preach that women were naturally evil and would seduce and debase men if they had the slightest opportunity. They then created a world in which women had to deny and suppress their own sexuality, resulting in indescribable frustration and suffering to the point that mental and physical ailments among women became common.

What all of the ancient world's alpha males and all of the religious clerics, ministers, popes, priests, shamans—or whatever they are called—misunderstood or ignored was the fundamental sexual nature of human beings.

Those misguided and gonad-driven males denied or ignored the fact that among all members of the animal kingdom, including human beings, sexuality comes right after survival in the built-in gene-powered drives. Furthermore, unlike some of their lower-order relatives male humans are "in heat" all the time. Females, on the other hand, want sex only on certain occasions and generally only with selected males.

Of course, there were enough valid social and political reasons for male leaders of early societies and religions to curb the sexual behavior of men and women. But the way they went about it was both inhuman and cruel. First of all, they put most of the responsibility on women, accusing them of not being able to control their sexual nature and therefore being a clear and present danger to society.

Religious Suppression of Female Sexuality

Throughout the history of Jewish, Christian, Islamic and other male-controlled societies virtually all women have been forced to suppress their natural sexuality to a degree which left them frustrated and subject to a variety of physical and mental ailments.

Remarkably, more than 2,000 years ago Hippocrates came up with the word "hysteria" to describe these ailments, but he didn't understand that they were caused by pent-up unused sexual energy.

Just as remarkable—given the ongoing ignorance of males and the influence of religions—in the 1880s an American doctor came up with the idea of using an electric vibrator as a medical treatment for women suffering from "female hysteria"—having somehow discovered that when the genitals of women suffering from "hysteria" were stimulated to orgasm the symptoms of the malady disappeared.

Even after the doctors discovered that orgasms eliminated this ancient "disease" neither they nor their patients realized that the cathartic release following genital stimulation had anything whatsoever to do with lack of sufficient sexual activity. They called it "paroxysm."

Despite the "sexual emancipation" of women that began in the United States in the early 20th century, picked up speed in the 1950s, and now often appears to be moving at the speed of light, most American women still today are constrained in their sexual behavior, repressing, ignoring or denying their sexuality to a significant degree.

With the "power of God" in their hands, male religious leaders long ago succeeded in brainwashing most women to not only accept the sexual restrictions placed on their behavior, but to also become firm believers in the righteousness of the laws—written and unwritten—that controlled their lives.

The Pope vs. Women

Over the centuries one of the most irrational and inhuman policies of the Catholic Church has been its prohibition of any form of artificial contraception, labeling it a grave sin against the will of God.

But finally, in an interview with a German journalist in 2010, Pope Benedict made the following deliberately convoluted comment: "There may be a basis in the case of some individuals, as perhaps when a male prostitute uses a condom, where this can be a first step in the direction of a moralization, a first assumption of responsibility."

This comment appears in a book entitled *Light of the World: The Pope, the Church and the Signs of the Times,* by Peter Seewald, released in November 2010. The Pope made the above comment when the journalist asked him if it wasn't "madness" for the Vatican to forbid a high-risk population from using condoms.

The Pope added that the Vatican does not regard the use of condoms by male prostitutes as a real or moral solution, and followed this with a weak-kneed comment that "it might be a first step in a movement toward a different way, a more human way, of living sexuality."

When asked about the Pope's unprecedented comments Catholic religious authorities said it was obviously a change in the ideology of the Vatican…a situation that once again exposed the irrationality and inhumanity of the traditional teachings of the Catholic Church.

One of the things that is forcing the Catholic Church to change its ways to avoid disappearing into the dustbins of history is the fact that thousands of priests have left and are leaving the Church in order to get married.

Fall-Out of the Primitive Male Mind

The gene-based need for males to dominate all areas of human endeavor resulted in selfish interests, tribalism, territorialism and discrimination against race, skin color and other religious beliefs becoming male characteristics.

Still today in many males these elements, separately or combined, override logic, objectivity and rationality in both subtle and obvious ways, resulting in behavior that is negative instead of positive, disruptive instead of harmonizing and destructive instead of constructive.

Examples of irrational, illogical and harmful behavior are so deeply ingrained in the minds of many males that they have become institutionalized and ritualized in customs and laws and have persisted since the dawn of human history...because the essential mindset of males has not changed and people with invested interests in the customs and laws have made sure that they continue to survive.

Humanity will continue to be plagued by ignorance, stupidity and violence as long as religious doctrines continue to preach and enforce the superiority of men and the inferiority of women, and prevent women from bringing their innate sense of compassion, cooperation and goodwill to the world at large.

Obviously, the sexual nature of males and the sex-based arrogance that led them to automatically assume that they were superior to females was to have results that went far beyond the oppression of females.

This arrogance and the cultural systems it created continue to plague mankind, and despite the examples of women who have ascended to power in the business and political worlds the underlying faults and failures of the religious-empowered syndrome remains in control in most societies.

The Female Revolution

Wise men and women have known for millennia that it is immoral and inhuman to treat women as the property of males, but it was not until the 19th century that women began to make their voices heard—and often went to jail for it.

It is absolutely incredible that male-created and dominated religious dogma prevented American women from having the right to vote until August 26, 1920, and still today many women around the world have far fewer political and social rights than men...all because of the hold that gender-based religions still have on the minds of people.

Women with few rights or virtually no rights at all have traditionally been brainwashed to accept the superiority of males and to be the most diligent followers of the very religions that have made them inferior creatures since day one.

But imagine what would happen if the vast majority of female Catholics, Christians, Jews and Muslims simply stopped going to and supporting the male-run churches, synagogues and mosques. Without female support, most of these institutions could not survive.

Ending of a Long Dark Age

Throughout recorded history there have been instances of women making major contributions to the cultures of ancient societies, including Chinese, Greek, Hindu and Persian. But these contributions virtually stopped with the ascendancy of the Christian religion and its large off-shoots, particularly Islam, which taught that females were inferior to males and morally fit only for child-bearing and serving men.

The rapid growth of Christianity between 33-93 A.D., Islam from around 650 A.D., and the orthodox Catholic version of Christianity from 1054 A.D.— much of it by force of arms—resulted in an educational Dark Age for most of the world's males until around the end of the 19th century and for most of the world's females until the middle of the 20th century.

For century after century all education was controlled by religions that preached and followed the doctrine that females are inferior to males and must be kept in their place, which included keeping them ignorant and submissive—a policy that still today is followed by a number of religions.

It was not until the early years of the 20th century that it became acceptable and possible for large numbers of American and European females to attend elementary level schools, and it was to be several more decades before female enrollment in colleges grew into significant numbers.

The emergence of females as the equals of males in the workplace [outside of farms] began in earnest in the United States during World War II in the mid-20th century, when factories and offices had no choice but to hire several million women to replace the men engaged in a male-made war.

This phenomenon alone did more than anything else to release most of the chauvinist-inspired and religious-enforced bonds that had kept American and European women down and submissive throughout history.

By the 1970s the number of American women in college, in managerial positions in industry and in politics had increased to the point that they were making their influence felt.

This number has continued to increase, and in some professions—health, for example—there are as many females as males, and in a few professional areas females outnumber males. U.S. medical schools are now graduating more female doctors than male doctors.

By the end of the first decade of the 21st century women in industry had reached the point that they were having a profound influence on management philosophy and practices, introducing policies that were gender neutral and took into account the special role that females play in keeping the species alive by having and nurturing babies.

However, the three areas that remained barely touched by female influence were religions, politics and education, all of which have been bastions of male power since the origin of these institutions.

Despite the fact that new technology combined with other changes in American culture—good and bad—have given females far more opportunities and power than they have ever had since the origin of the species, their unique female mindset—so different from the male mind—has just begun to bring about fundamental changes in the institutions and enterprises that control American life.

It is, in fact, remarkable that the more outgoing and aggressive American females become the *more feminine American males become*—but the meeting of the two genders in a rational and positive compromise is still far away.

Ultimately, the genetic factor that nails the superiority of the female sex is that when women are free to think and behave in a way that is natural for them they are intrinsically more practical, more logical, more rational, and more humane than males—all factors that are essential parts of the make-up of females because they are responsible for the actual creation and nurturing of human life.

If you make up a list of all of the cruel, destructive, evil, inhumane, savage and stupid things that have happened to human beings—and are, of course, still happening today—at least 95 percent of the people responsible for these things have been and are males.

The world desperately needs a new universal cultural paradigm that is devoid of theological-based myths and ignorance, and is based instead on the positive potential of the human species—a potential that now includes actually becoming god-like in the ability to do good…or evil.

The trouble with the world
is that the stupid are cocksure
and the intelligent are full of doubt!

—Bertrand Russell—

[8]
The Failure of God-Based Moralities

The specific reasons for the failure of virtually every aspect of human cultures include gender differences and male-oriented and male-directed moralities.

The single most important factor in the overall failure of human cultures has, in fact, been male dominance. The second most important factor has been the influence of male-dominated religions, including Judaism, Christianity and Islam, all of which embody the worst characteristics of cults—a cult, by definition, being a system of community or religious worship and ritual, especially one focusing upon a single deity or spirit; an obsessive devotion or veneration for a person, principle or ideal; an exclusive group of people sharing an esoteric interest.

One of the original fundamental flaws in God-based Judaism, Christianity and Islam religions was divorcing the mind from the physical body; completely separating the needs of the body from the aspirations for a divine spiritual existence and eternal life…a concept that brought some comfort to ignorant humanity but the suffering it has caused is immeasurable.

It is, of course, an obvious and indisputable fact that man-made religious moralities have not succeeded in creating peace and goodwill among human beings. Every form of violence and ill-will imaginable is as common today, if not more so, than at any time in the history of the species.

The Forked-Tongue of God's Spokesmen

The daily news is rife with references to God that are so irrational they go beyond being ridiculous. Clerics, preachers, terrorists, politicians, military men and others are constantly calling on God to bless them and their countries, and to bring death and destruction to their enemies.

There are other destructive mental and moral aberrations across the board in societies where the guidelines for human behavior are based on an irrational male-oriented theological concept, with so-called entertainment being one of the most conspicuous examples.

It is also incredible that much of modern-day entertainment—one of the biggest and most culturally influential of all industries—is based on catering to the most primitive, savage and gross side of humanity. The Christian Church in particular cannot compete with this form of mass cultural conditioning.

The Bill of Rights Virus

In fact, the Bill of Rights attached to the American Constitution forbids both the government and religious institutions from interfering with the public expression of the most gross and dehumanizing elements of "freedom of speech."

This black hole of immorality has come about in part because over the decades the laws of the United

States have been skewered by ideologue politicians and other politicians under pressure from business leaders and others to favor and permit the debasement of humanity for the sake of profit—and most people at large accept this situation for a variety of reasons: they tell themselves they can't change it; that it is not their responsibility, and so on. It is also obvious that many people who publicly oppose this pandemic of profit-oriented cultural sleaze are strongly attracted to it.

The goal in producing and marketing sleaze is, of course, to make a profit. And the reason it is so profitable is because the attempts of religions and secular societies to control human behavior, despite their good intentions, have created a hunger for sleaze in all of its forms...especially those that are sex-related. Feeding this obsession drives the behavior of a large percentage of humanity.

Over the millennia many wise men and women have tried to replace religions with a philosophy of life that does not depend upon male-created gods but on simple common-sense universal rules and guidelines based on what is good and best for all humans. But just as obviously these attempts have failed because the intellect of most human beings has not yet evolved to the point that people can transcend the religious moralities of the cultures they are raised in—or on their own overcome their built-in tendencies to think and behave in irrational and destructive ways.

It goes without saying that children are not capable of preventing themselves from being programmed like robots by their environment. To varying degrees they learn and accept the ways of their parents and other adults in their society—or they face a variety of punishments that range from being criticized, shamed and ostracized to—in some countries—being mutilated or murdered by their own fathers, brothers or other male adults.

It is true, of course, that Judaism, Christianity and Islam were founded with the best of intentions but it was not long before they were turned into instruments of discrimination, oppression, violence and murder. Throughout their history mayhem and war have been among their primary legacies to mankind.

Over the millennia the vast majority of people who have accepted and attempted to live by the precepts of man-made religions—in other words, to live morally upright lives according to the precepts of their particular religion—have been the least powerful, the most down-trodden and the most victimized by the state and by the church…in other words, women.

In societies with god-based religions the word God itself has been turned into a catchall term that is used to justify murder by individuals and mass-killing by states. Pathological killers as well as the most upright members of societies beseech God to aid them in the destruction of their competitors and enemies, and praise God when they succeed.

That this incongruity is ignored by many of those who profess to believe in and follow the precepts of a "loving God" is pathological to the extreme. To be more precise, it is a form of cultural insanity. In virtually the same breath "God the Creator and Savior" becomes "God the Avenger, the Destroyer and the Bringer of Death" to one's enemies and disbelievers.

In human history good and bad have never existed in reality as fixed polar opposites. They have always been circumstantial and were whatever was prescribed at the time by the ruling powers—the clergy, the government and the military, or whichever one of these entities was dominant. These three institutions have also traditionally worked hand-in-hand to indoctrinate, subjugate and control people for their own purposes.

It goes without saying that for the vast majority of people survival and some degree of security and comfort take precedence over all other things. And if professing to believe in something like Islam, for example, will provide this security and comfort, even to a small degree, people programmed in that faith will believe and obey even the most irrational and inhuman dogma.

When the United States was founded some of the teachings of Christianity that are humane, positive and nurturing were incorporated into the laws of the land. But institutionalized Christianity was not made a state religion because it was clearly seen as an enemy of intellectual and personal freedom.

Other Reasons Why God-Based Moralities Have Failed

People in God-oriented societies commonly behave in ways that are contrary to religious teachings—in many cases because the teachings range from being impractical to inhuman, dangerous or worse, and following them makes no sense.

The concept that the "Kingdom of Heaven" is *within* the individual—not in some after-death Heaven high in the sky—is probably the most important of all of the insights attributed to the historical Jesus as well as many other earlier philosophers like Confucius. But it goes against the teachings of Judaism, Christianity and Islam, all of which hold that God is the *only* source of wisdom and proper behavior—by which they mean what these male-dominated cults teach.

In fact, according to the teachings of Christianity you can "sin" left and right and still go to Heaven if you confess and accept Jesus Christ [God manifested in the flesh to save mankind!], as your savior before you die—an incredible cop-out devised by religious leaders in an effort to make god-based religion more attractive to the masses.

Judaism, Christianity and Islam have never had all of the right answers for the spiritual needs of humanity—as history has so graphically demonstrated. Now, more and more so-called Christians are creating their own personal paths to fulfilling their spiritual needs.

And then, of course, some two-thirds of the world's population is *not* Christian or Jew—even if in name only. These are the Muslims, the Buddhists, the Hindus, and so on—most of whom have had good reason for disliking and fearing Christianity because of its intolerant claim of exclusivity and historical use of violence...not to mention the primitive, irrational elements of its theology.

India-American physician, author and public speaker Dr. Deepak Chopra has presented a succinct explanation of the difference between religion and spirituality. He reminds people that religions develop long after the occurrence of spiritual experiences. He notes that Jesus Christ was not a Christian and Buddha was not a Buddhist. "Those religious were ultimately constructed around an ideology, and of necessity took on the rigidity and risk of being taken over by people who were more interested in power-mongering and corruption. Spirituality, on the other hand, is a realm of awareness that is universal and goes beyond dogma."

Spirituality does indeed have a vital role to play in human life, but it has not been rationally presented by Judaism, Christianity or Islam—all of which were created by ignorant men who were beset by sexism, tribalism and racism that adversely affected their efforts to control human behavior.

In more ways than one, the God-based moralities of Judaism, Christianity and Islam have become an unfunny joke. The daily news is rife with references to God that are so irrational they go beyond being ridiculous.

Interestingly, Dennis Prager, the Jewish-American author and commentator on personal and social issues from morality to religion, has said that most present-day Israelis are not religious in their day-to-day behavior. That is also true, of course, of most Christian Americans, most of whom are too busy living.

Recent surveys of American Christians reveal that the Christianity they profess to believe in is little more than a cultural brand—not a testament to their beliefs or behavior.

The Anti-Female Catholic Religion

One of the most incredible continuing failings of the Catholic version of Christianity is the Vatican's position on women in the Church. Near the end of the 20th century a number of groups of Catholics who had distanced themselves from the rigid orthodoxy of the

Vatican began to give women roles that had previously been the absolute preserves of males.

Some of these steps involved ordaining women as priests, a move that drew quick condemnation from the Vatican. In 2010 when break-away Catholic Churches ordained a number of female priests the move resulted in the Vatican condemning the action *as a grave sin on a par with the sexual abuse of children.* Incredible!

A spokesperson for the Vatican explained the position of the Church as following the precedent set by Jesus Christ who, the spokesperson said, remained celibate all his life and ordained only males who had been baptized into the priesthood.

The bishop in charge later excommunicated a male priest who was involved in ordaining a female as a priest. The bishop explained his action by saying: *"Actions such as these are extremely serious and carry with them profoundly harmful consequences for the salvation of souls participating in this attempted ordination."*

That was an incredibly stupid, anti-human, anti-female thing for a high-ranking member of the Catholic Church to say, and it obviously represented the official position of the Church.

To permanently condemn one-half of humanity as inferior to males and not worthy of acting on behalf of the Church to teach moral behavior is an astounding example of the primitive mindset of both the male founders and present-day leaders of the Catholic Church—not to mention Islam, which is even more anti-female.

The chauvinistic and anti-human practices of the male-dominated Catholic and Islamic Churches have, of course, been the rule since day one and until modern times the power of the Church was such that women did not dare to question it. But until the power of the Church to defy common sense and to ignore the humanity it professes to hold sacred is broken it will continue to discriminate against women.

Why the Catholic Church has been able to maintain its power for such a long time is not a secret. Most males in the most "Catholic countries" have simply ignored the dogma and dictates of the Church in their normal "week-day" behavior—that has included cheating, lying, engaging in promiscuous sexual behavior and various forms and degrees of violence, most often against women.

As one honest Filipino Catholic priest once noted, "There is Catholic morality and there is Reality. Except when they go to Church on Sundays most Catholic laymen live in the world of Reality."

Until the fundamental errors that are built into the foundations of the largest and most powerful religions are acknowledged and corrected by their male rulers they will continue to be a major part of the failure of human beings to achieve even a small portion of their potential.

But given the pathological mentality of the Christian and Islamic Church lords this reformation will not happen until the religions are on the verge of becoming totally obsolete simply because the people at large will stop blindly supporting them.

Now that religions are no longer able to oppress people with impunity the gradual weakening of their hold on the mindset of well over half of humanity is, in fact, inevitable. Their "sins" are quickly made public.

It is becoming obvious to more and more people that the salvation of humanity lies in rational, factual education; not in male-created and male-dominated religious cults—and again if you question the reference to Judaism, Christianity and Islam as cults look up the word cult in your dictionary.

Religions Live on Ignorance

From their inceptions all of the branches of Judaism, Christianity and Islam have been based on ignorance—on the simple fact that people knew virtually nothing about the cosmos, the solar system, the Earth, the existence of thousands of other societies on other continents, and so on. And it was this prevailing ignorance over the centuries that made it possible for these religions to survive and thrive.

Not surprisingly, much of this ignorance in all of these religious sects still prevails today despite the fact that mankind has walked on the moon, astronomers study the billions of galaxies and more billions of stars in the cosmos, and scientists can literally create life.

What is equally sad is that long before the appearance of Christianity and Islam ancient Sumerian and Greek scholars and scientists had actually deduced that the Earth is a globe that is in orbit around the sun; had identified all of the inner planets out to Saturn; and had deduced that human beings evolved from lower life forms going all the way back to fish!—all knowledge lost or ignored by the time these religions were created.

A 2010 poll by the prestigious *Pew Forum on Religion & Public Life* revealed that still today American Roman Catholics and Protestants actually know very little about the history and basic tenets of their own faith. The survey revealed that atheists, agnostics, Jews and Mormons knew more about religious dogma than Catholics and Protestants.

While the United States is commonly referred to as one of the most religious nations in the world, the facts are that most Americans are ignorant not only about their own particular brand of faith they know even less about other faiths. And also not surprisingly, the lower the level of education of the individual the less he or she knew about religion. And here is a good kicker: atheists and agnostics scored the highest on the survey questions. Catholics scored the lowest.

The Willful Stupidity Element!

One should be able to assume that present-day leaders of most religions are neither stupid nor ignorant. Even though most of them have been raised within the restraints and taboos of their particular church and have been programmed by their environment and pro-fessional studies to accept the teachings of their par-ticular religion, it requires a great deal of willful stupidity for them to deny what they see and hear in the real world, and in what their intrinsic common sense tells them.

While some of the motives of many of the clergy in all religions may be pure and positive, continuing to pursue beliefs and practices that are patently false, invalid and anti-human requires a twisted mind. That is willful stupidity taken to the extreme.

The news media recently carried interviews with two life-long religious pastors who admitted that they no longer believed in the existence of God—or any god for that matter. And how did they say they came to this startling insight? They said they did so by actually reading the Bible and discovering that it is primarily based on stories written by men totally ignorant of the nature, scope and grandeur of the cosmos attempting to prove there is a God who can and does break every law of nature but never actually does anything at all to save mankind from itself.

In simple terms, religious clergy have been brainwashed by their teachers and mentors and their overall environment—or they dupe themselves for some ulterior reason. Or they are perfectly aware of the duplicity of their position and actions and continue for reasons that have nothing to do with "saving souls."

Most of the world's religions have traditionally depended upon one thing to keep their uneducated members coming back for more. Fear! Fear that they will be condemned to Hell if they don't profess to believe and go through the prescribed rituals; and fear of the reprisals their Church and fellow members will take against them in this life if they don't conform to the prescribed behavior.

In earlier times reprisals by the Catholic Church ranged from being ostracized and shamed to being tortured and killed, often in the most horrible ways imaginable. In modern times the Church has moderated its punishment to social sanctions and the threat of eternal Hell instead of some form of execution.

Of course, the vast majority of Muslims are as non-violent and as tolerant as the average Christians and Jews but radical Islamic clerics remain hung up on the primitive beliefs and customs that were common when Islam was founded in the 7th century A.D.

Teaching children that they are going to burn in Hell forever if they don't obey the dictates of any religion is pathological, and so far from the original intent of religions that it is criminal. Prevailing upon young men and women to strap bombs to their bodies to seek out and kill as many people as possible in a struggle for religious and political power goes beyond pathology.

When the mothers of these brainwashed assassins say on camera how proud they are of their martyred sons and daughters it is unreal. It is even more unreal when it is discovered that the terrorists paid the families of the assassins. Only rational, non-religious education can cure this inhuman insanity.

The Life is Sacred Nonsense!

Another example of the nonsensical and dangerous influences of the combination of the male mind and religion is the concept that life is sacred. People in cultures that have been profoundly influenced by the Judeo-Christian God concept have been taught that life is sacred, and that only God can legitimately give and take life—human life, that is, since God (it is said) gave mankind dominion over all other life forms (otherwise we would not be able to kill and eat animals, fish, fowls and a variety of other forms of life without committing a sin).

The idea that a living god created all life—especially human life—and that life is sacred is so transparently invalid that it should have made any continuing belief in the concept patently impossible. And yet it is still one of the primary teachings of Judaism, Christianity and Islam.

The life-is-sacred myth is, of course, a concept created by the founders of Judaism and Christianity in an attempt to wean males away from their instincts to mistreat and kill others and to reprogram them to be respectful, kind and cooperative. In the eyes of these ancient founders only a god would be capable of such a miracle, and rightly so.

However, the primitive destructive instincts of human males were so strong that just being told that life was sacred was not enough to suppress these instincts in many men, with the result that mayhem and murder have continued to be a distinguishing characteristic of humanity.

In fact, not long after the creation of the life-is-sacred concept, religious leaders themselves began to use violence in the name of their God in an attempt to force others to believe as they did and to obey the rules they had devised in an effort to control all thinking and behavior.

Incredibly, according to the Bible when Moses came down from Mt. Sinai with the first 10 Commandments and found that large numbers of his followers had created and were worshipping a golden calf and having a hell of a good time, he was so incensed that he smashed the stone tablet bearing the Commandments and ordered his faithful followers to kill those who had stayed from the path. In one of the worst massacres in history his followers slaughtered over 3,000 fellow Jews—men, women and children. Moses then went back up on Mt. Sinai and [it is said] and had God use his finger to rewrite the 10 Commandments on another stone slab!

Life is indeed precious to most human beings, but the history of humanity demonstrates that there is absolutely nothing sacred about it. Those who continue to profess belief in the sacred concept merely demonstrate that the human mind can be manipulated like any computer soft-ware program, and when confronted with reality they resort to claiming it is a matter of faith, not facts or reality.

It is apparently the cosmos itself that is the Great Creator. It is infused with an inherent force to create life in forms and functions that are seemingly countless...in environments that are incredibly diverse and extreme. On Earth, new forms of life are discovered almost daily as scientists and others probe deeper into the oceans, into the subterranean depths of the Earth, and into isolated places on the surface of the Earth. One of these days we will discover that life in varying forms is common among the billions of planets circling billions of stars.

Regardless of the form and function of any life form, in whatever environment, life to that particular form is precious, but, again, it is not sacred. All life forms, including humans, are subject to being obliterated, often in an instant, by other life forms and by nature.

Life is, in fact, based on life forms killing and eating other life forms—a food chain that is exactly the opposite of the religious concept that life is sacred. Nature creates life and life destroys life in order to survive and grow and become more adept at devouring other forms of life (not counting incidents of human cannibalism, of course).

The religious concept that is life is sacred crops up in virtually all areas of human life, and is routinely ignored by the majority. Opponents of abortions use the life-is-sacred argument to proclaim that abortions are a sin against God. This dumb argument is also used by people who oppose the use of human stem cells in medical research.

Going one step farther, this rationale would apply to female eggs [most of which are disposed of naturally] and male sperm, most of which goes to "waste." As already noted, there is an injunction in the Bible that describes masturbation as a grave sin, and states that "It is better to leave your seed in the belly of a whore than to cast it to the wind." How's that for a pithy summation of religious morality!

As stated, virtually all organic life forms on Earth exist by killing and eating other life forms—or in many cases eating them while they are *still alive*—in which case they are commonly promoted in some cultures as special treats. Now, only humans are normally not on the food chain… but don't turn your back on an alligator or any other really big lizard!

The Abortion Controversy!

An abortion can, of course be a dangerous and ignoble thing for a woman to go through, but done early enough and safely enough it is often a better choice than to have an unplanned, unwanted child. Being forced to have an unplanned and unwanted child—especially one that cannot be properly cared for and educated—because of an ancient and primitive religious belief is simply not rational; not right.

People who oppose abortions should spend their time and energy in helping women avoid unwanted pregnancies in the first place. There are millions of women around the world who are in desperate need of such help and every year they produce millions more children, many of whose lives are short and wretched.

As contradictory as it often is, human beings are the most advanced form of life known and some humans are capable of creating masterpieces of art, architecture, literature, music and technological marvels. In many areas, scientists and technicians are literally transforming life itself in "god-like" ways. And yet, large numbers of human beings are still driven by the instincts of their primitive ids to use force, to repress, to maim and murder to get what they want. This destructive behavior, on an individual as well as on group and national levels, is often done in the name of their God.

There is obviously a great deal of good in cultures influenced by Judaism, Christianity and Islam, but the myths and myopia these religions spawn and the irrational behavior they often justify continue to bring immeasurable suffering, destruction and death to millions of people.

To repeat, the irrational position that abortion is a sin against God because life is sacred is simply nonsense. It is a deplorable answer to the irresponsibility of a male and a female—most often a male. There are other answers!

The Rebellion of Catholic Women

The sex-and-gender obsessed Catholic Church has been losing American members and priests since the political emancipation of women began in the 20th century, but it was not until female members of the cult began a concerted rebellion against its sexist practices near the end of the century that dissension within the ranks became big time.

The really Big Bang occurred in 2010 as a result of the Vatican's reaction when a number of new female priests were ordained in the U.S. and in Europe. The Vatican declared that in the eyes of God women were unfit to be priests and that ordaining them was a grave sin on the same level as the sexual abuse of young boys by priests.

In the new connected world of the Internet that absurd sexist reaction went viral within hours, resulting in the publication of data showing that most American Catholics disagree with the Vatican's anti-female views and are in favor of ordaining women.

One summary of the rebellion against the doctrines of the Church suggested that the male lords would eventually abolish the edict that male priests could not marry in an attempt to remain a relevant power in the lives of people, but the summary did not foresee the day when the Church would accept females into its male-dominated hierarchy.

That is inevitable if the Catholic Church is to survive—but in the long run it will be better for humanity if it does not survive as long as it continues to preach that a God is—or should be—in charge of everything.

[9]
PROFIT AS THE NEW GOD

The Rise of Money Morality

The fact that Judaism, Christianity and Islam failed in their self-declared mandates to control human behavior allowed the rise of a new morality that is even more destructive—a new morality that was fueled by the Industrial Revolution that began in England in the early 1800s and was to have more far-reaching effects on human history than any other element since the development of agriculture and the creation of god-based religions.

One of the most important of these effects was that the new economy that developed over the next century was centered on profit-making as the new imperative of all businesses and government organizations, and *earning money* was the new imperative of the people who worked for them.

During the early 19th century money-and-profit-making became the economic, social and political foundations of the industrialized countries of the West. By the beginning of the 20th century all of the domestic and international affairs of the newly industrialized countries were based on the new money morality.

The perceived and real need for economic expansion, both to meet growing populations and the hunger for more economic and political power, resulted in wars becoming an even more vital aspect of public policy in a number of countries.

Among the first of these economic wars was the invasion and colonization of most of Southeast Asia and big chunks of China by European countries. In the early 1900s Japan joined the fray by invading and colonizing Korea. Then came World War I and World War II, both started by Germany to expand its economic and political clout, with Japan soon following the German example by invading China, Southeast Asia and islands in the Pacific.

At present, most of the conflicts among industrialized nations are economic rather than military. But killing and other savage actions continue on a grand scale in some countries—despite efforts by the United Nations and individual nations to stop them.

No matter how many reasons one can come up with to explain this violence the ultimate cause lies in the lack of the right kind of practical and moral education—education that programs people in the common-sense attributes that are the foundation of peace, goodwill, tolerance and co-operation in improving the welfare of all—all things god-based religions have failed to do.

There is virtually no area of human endeavor, including the survival and activities of religious institutions, that is not based on or does not depend on money. Technology could alter this dependence but that is a long way off, given the relationship between money, politics and power.

The Excess-Consumption Time Bomb!

The profit motive has not only replaced religious-based moralities it has created an excess-consumption syndrome that is socially and spiritually insane and is like a cancer eating away at humanity and inflicting irreparable harm to the Earth.

The areas of human consumption in industrialized societies that are the most abused by the compulsion to make a profit—and are the most damaging to both humanity and the Earth—include fossil-based energy, military armaments, fashion-based wearing apparel, drugs, processed foodstuffs, alcoholic beverages, tobacco products and sugar-laden drinks.

The damage done not only to the human psyche and societies in general but also to the Earth by promoting excess consumption of these and other products is incalculable in both spiritual and material terms.

This mindless drive to make a profit based on excess consumption results in most of the imagination and creative talent of mankind being used to promote the sales of products in volumes that are not related in any way to the actual needs of people.

More and more people are recognizing the stupidity and immorality of this kind of culture, but only a few have the intestinal fortitude in the first place to not fall prey to the blandishments of advertising and a social image that publicly proclaims their success in making more money than what they need to live modestly. Fewer still willingly give it up after they are caught up in the conspicuous consumption syndrome.

Americans created this lifestyle and mentality, and like a disease it has spread to other countries, particularly the newly developed and still developing countries, with China being an outstanding example.

What is incredible about the rise of China and the problems of the United States is that the Chinese approach to education, the economy and international trade as expounded by Premier Wen Jiabao in 2010 was more rational and intelligent—if self-serving—than the American approach...a phenomenon recorded by Fareed Zakaria, an editor of *Time* magazine, following an interview of Wen.

Zakaria noted that the policies the Chinese leadership has followed since the 1980s have included building new colleges and universities, dramatically increasing the number of graduates in math and science and building an infrastructure that includes state-of-the-art airports, highways and a high-speed train network—all key parts of modernizing and internationalizing China's economy. He added that the education network the Chinese created in less than a decade is the largest in the world—an expansion Yale University President Richard Levin described as without precedent.

Just as American business and government leaders ignored the fantastic economic progress Japan made between 1950 and 1970—during which it became the world's second largest economy—they at first ignored the fact that China began taking exactly the same steps in the late 1970s.

What an incredible example of the myopia and willful stupidity of American leaders in all fields! The once despised Chinese Communist leaders giving

Americans a lesson in capitalism! And by the end of the first decade of the 21st century China was already in the midst of its second giant leap forward: the creation of a mass market that could eventually encompass over one billion people—a phenomenon that will have far more impact on the world than the rise of Japan.

But in creating their own economic juggernaut the Chinese leaders seem to have forgotten some of the other sage wisdom of Lao Tzu, who almost three thousand years ago wrote: "When man interferes with nature the sky becomes filthy, the Earth becomes depleted, harmony with nature disappears, and creatures become extinct."

Japan was the first Asian nation to develop a mass market-based economy—between 1950 and 1965—a remarkable event chronicled in 1967 in the book, *The Japanese as Consumers—Asia's First Mass Market*, written by this author and Fred Thomas Perry.

Japan was also the first Asian nation to fall prey to the excess consumption syndrome; a cultural switch of extraordinary importance because up to 1960 the Japanese had maintained an austere but physically, emotionally and spiritually balanced life-style for over two thousand years.

This early unique Japanese lifestyle evolved from precepts contained in Shintō, their native religion, which taught respect and reverence for nature; for beauty simplified and refined down to its essence; the avoidance of conspicuous excess display, and the presence of harmony in design and style as well as in behavior.

The traditional lifestyle of the Japanese has been maintained in many areas, including shops dealing in traditional arts and crafts, restaurants featuring traditional foods, and traditional *ryokan* [rio-kahn] or inns, which still abound in the country. But for the majority of the Japanese it has been replaced by the American or Western style of living.

However, before the turn of the 21st century a growing number of Japanese began to suffer from a cultural malaise brought on by the mass consumption lifestyle, resulting in them going at least part of the way back to the simple way of living that had sustained them for millennia. For some, this included moving out of crowded urban areas into the countryside.

The whole industrialized world is challenged to follow this example to some extent—overcoming the excess-consumption syndrome and returning to a more balanced and satisfying lifestyle. This movement, although tiny, is growing in the United States, albeit slowly. Much of the future of the world depends on what China will do.

It should not be surprising to Westerns caught up in mass consumption that the foundation of Japan's traditional lifestyle was emotional and spiritual harmony; the antithesis of mass consumption.

While it is inconceivable that large numbers of affluent Americans and other Westerners would give up their wasteful and discordant lifestyles readily and easily, it nevertheless is one way that would return commonsense and harmony to their lives, and there are signs that this movement is growing.

If you are interested in learning more about the foundation of Japan's traditional culture, see **ELEMENTS OF JAPANESE DESIGN – Understanding and Using Japan's Classic Wabi-Sabi-Shibui Concepts.**

The New Drug Lords

The multi-billion-dollar-a-year drug industry in the U.S., both legal and illegal, has become an economic, political and social issue that is a frightening and dangerous example of the failure of basic parental responsibility, teacher responsibility, government responsibility, industry responsibility, news media responsibility, and more.

The movement toward a drug-addicted society began with the Hippie phenomenon of the 1960s and from then on was promoted by news media coverage and the movie and music industries.

By 2010 the market for illegal drugs in the U.S. had spawned a war in Mexico, pitting drug cartels against the government—a war that the government was incapable of winning, resulting in it beginning to consider legalizing recreational drug use—a concept highly criticized by those who pointed out that it was the market for drugs in the U.S. that fueled and financed the Mexican drug cartels.

In the United States the movement to legalize marijuana was making dramatic inroads under the guise of "medical marijuana"—a movement headed by the Medical Marijuana Project, a lobbying and information group based in Washington, D.C. that was both insidious and clever in presenting the benefits of thousands of new marijuana drugstores across the country.

Again, it was money that drove this movement, not concern for people who had illnesses that cause permanent pain. And because dealing in drugs is extremely profitable there was no lack of money to finance the campaign.

Listening to proponents of medical marijuana— those in government as well as those on the outside— one could assume that legalizing medical pot was an opportunity to create thousands of good-paying jobs and bring large amounts of tax dollars into city and state coffers.

Some Arizona politicians who were asked about the push to legalize medical marijuana suggested that it might be a good idea for the dispensaries to be run by the state. Others suggested that the dispensaries should be associated with pharmacies and other medical providers. Arizona voters approved the sale of "medical pot" in the state in 2010.

The first states to approve of medical marijuana dispensaries were California in 1996; Alaska, Oregon and Washington in 1998 and Maine in 1999. All people need to buy pot legally in states where it has been approved is a note from a doctor saying they would benefit from it. Doctors get paid for passing out these prescriptions.

Given the legal production and sale of alcohol and nicotine products it seems inevitable that marijuana will be legalized by tax-hungry states.

When the use of marijuana, heroin, meth and other drugs are added to the vast and still growing array of legal drugs sold in the United States the total is staggering. Several million people of all ages, including children, are on daily dosages of prescribed drugs... many of which have no beneficial effect whatsoever and some of which have serious side-effects.

Referring to the national epidemic of pill popping, *TIME* magazine labeled the "well-intentioned" use of drugs prescribed by regular doctors as "Addiction by Prescription."

It goes without saying that both the legal and illegal drug industries are profit-and-growth-driven...the new American morality.

There is no end to the reach and influence of the profit motive in American life. It permeates and prevails in virtually everything we do outside of pure charity work, overriding commonsense and any pretense of morality.

The health insurance industry's stealth campaign to prevent health care reform, carried out by some of the country's top public relations pros on behalf of their corporate clients, was an example of the power of businesses to preserve their profit margins at the expense of the people they claim to serve.

Religion as a Profit-Making Business

The Catholic Church in particular is a huge commercial and political enterprise more concerned with profit and growth—and keeping males on top—than with the spiritual lives of its members.

In fact, the Catholic Church has been more interested in profits and politics than in truth and in the quality of life since before the Middle Ages, but it was only with the dramatic increase in knowledge and the educational level of the laity that the Church began to lose spiritual relevance. The Pope and his huge staff of generals have become business managers, more interested in profit-and-loss than in convincing members that they will go to Heaven when they die if they follow the ancient dictates and continue to finance the Church.

The loss of religion-based morality in business, politics and society in general—as inhuman and as discriminatory as it always has been—was nevertheless a real loss because it at least had some standards of conduct for people in charge that sometimes benefitted those without power.

Now, there is no area of human endeavor that is not controlled by the profit motive, and more often than not profit takes precedence over any abstract religious morality that has survived. This includes education and politics in addition to every category of business.

Well before the turn of the 21st century the rise of the profit morality had become even more complicated because of the increasing international demand for oil and raw materials to feed the insatiable maws of modern life.

The Foreign Affairs Dilemma

As is well known, all industrially advanced countries that do not have sufficient oil, iron ore, copper and a various other raw materials now compete with each other politically as well as economically.

This has resulted in a situation in which profit-oriented have-nots are essentially hostages to the haves, creating a foreign affairs dilemma for many nations, especially the U.S., for which there are no fast, easy solutions.

War, which has traditionally been the solution to such problems, is no longer an easy option. Having to deal with rogue, unfriendly nations that are major suppliers of oil or other critical resources makes the problems even more complicated.

Contemplating what this could mean for mankind on a short-term is not a pleasant experience. But the bright side of this dilemma is that it is forcing leaders to talk instead of fight, and is encouraging them to do the things they should have been doing anyway at least for decades if not centuries—and that, of course, is developing new benign sources of energy, creating new green products and developing a green lifestyle.

The optimistic view is that there is enough innate goodness in most of humanity that when the huge mass of ordinary people reach the mindset that things must change, and achieve the ability to force these changes on those in power, a universal morality that is rational, logical, practical and beneficial will emerge.

There are going to be many dark decades before that happens, but there is hope. In addition to wind and solar power there is also the probability that oil produced from algae and other green sources could supplement power needs until efforts to harness energy from nuclear fusion becomes a reality.

When oil is replaced by other energy sources, the changes that will occur in politics and economics could be as fundamental as discovering how to make and control fire.

In an odd twist of fate, the only profit-making competitor that is even more powerful than oil is pornography. It is easy and cheap to produce, and can be distributed around the world in one second, at virtually no cost.

[10]
The Black Hole of Politics

The basic political system in the United States was created in a time when the overall population of the country was tiny, the number of eligible voters was smaller still, and there were far fewer power groups with their own agendas. If people really didn't like what was going on in their districts they could simply load up and move west where at first there were no political processes at all. As time passed and the populations grew money began to play an increasing role in the political system.

By the beginning of the 20th century the new money morality had infected and corrupted American culture and the political process from top to bottom. As is so glaringly obvious today people who want to participate in the governing process must buy their way into office.

Individuals running for offices who are not wealthy must raise thousands to millions of dollars to finance their campaigns. One of the most conspicuous ex-amples of this occurred in 2010. That year the candidate for the governorship of California, Meg Whitman, former CEO of eBay, spent $141 million of her own money and another $25 million in donations—

apparently the record for any political candidate in the history of the country; topping 2008 presidential candidate Mitt Romney, who spent $115 million during the primary elections campaign that year (and lost). Whitman also lost.

That was an incredible travesty of the original political system, and a glaring example of the depths to which American culture had sunk.

By the summer of 2010 the level of political competition for power had reached new heights of immoral absurdity—a phenomenon advanced by an advertising "genius" whose forte was creating advertisements based on statements and images that were so shocking they were raw red meat for the online news media, resulting in them going viral in a matter of minutes, bringing his clients millions of dollars worth of publicity and making them virtually instant "celebrities."

This genius simply took advantage of the fact that the more outrageous an ad the more attention it will get, regardless of how inaccurate or how stupid it might be—the point being that enough of the public would end up voting for the candidates to maybe get them elected. What this had to stay about the moral character of the political figures who agreed to this approach is a good question.

The American political system is not going to reform itself. First, in most states the division of counties into political districts—which is the prerogative of state legislators—is obsolete, impractical, inefficient, unfair, undemocratic and irrational, and the system should be abolished.

Failure of the Committee System

The political-party system of government as practiced in the United States is virtually bankrupt. One of its worst elements is the committee system, which has a profound influence on who gets what done. In addition to different ideologies that divide committee members on both state and federal levels the party in power gets to select the chairmen in control of the committees.

This means that instead of being a good example of the democratic process, individual committee chairmen can decide on what and when to bring up issues and they and their fellow party members almost always vote as a block.

Junior congressmen and senators who have promised their constituents that they are going to reform Washington politics when they get there have virtually no power even when appointed to committees because they generally must do the bidding of the senior party members whether they agree with them or not.

One of the first lessons that newcomers in Congress learn is that they must spend the bulk of their time raising funds for the next election.

The committee system virtually guarantees that most of the legislation introduced by members—old and new, and especially new members—goes directly into a black hole and never sees the light of day. Actually, given the purpose and quality of much of the legislation that is not all bad!

The committee system primarily serves the interest of a few and given the built-in egoism of those in power they are not likely to change it.

Two New Branches of Government!

The political system in the United States today has morphed into a kind of multi-headed monster that mitigates against common sense and rational, focused behavior. One of the reasons for this is the appearance of two new un-official branches of government that are not by the people or for the people.

These are the far left and the far right elements of the news media and the lobbyists—both individual lobbyist who must register and account for the money they spend, and the far more powerful corporate entities from non-profits to unions that do not have to register as lobbyists and over which there are no restraints on how much money they can use to buy political influence.

The combination of the dark sides of these two un-official branches of government poisons the political atmosphere and prevents the legal branches of government from doing the job they were designed to do.

In goes without saying that these unofficial branches of government are not going to change their spots or their behavior. It is also obvious that the influence of the lobby branch is so powerful that elected officials cannot legislate it out of business—although efforts have been made to rein it in.

That leaves it up to untainted public officials, journalists and the public at large to identify and expose the individuals, companies and organizations that have usurped the legitimate powers of the government to the point that they become ineffective and wither away. Good luck on that!

Ideological Conflicts

American voters are so spoiled they demand instant, painless fixes by the government to problems that have been in the making for decades while at the same time shouting that Big Government is the problem and should be dramatically downsized, resulting in candidates and incumbents alike promising fixes they cannot deliver because the government does not have that kind of control over the causes of the problems.

Past attempts by the government to fix old economic problems and avoid creating new ones have resulted in an infrastructure of entitlements, rules and regulations that have created more problems than they have solved, are unsustainable, and are unfixable in the present political climate. Again referring to Lao Tzu, the ancient Chinese sage, he said that the more laws and rules created by leaders the more people will break them.

The reason the problems cannot be fixed is that the ideological fault lines between the old and new political parties are so wide and deep, and the self-interest of the committee and party leaders is so powerful, they refuse to compromise their positions, much less accept a good idea advanced by the other party.

Not surprisingly, one of the major sources of ideological conflicts within the political parties are the divisions between those who want more religion in government and those who favor a totally secular government. What is politically correct for one side is political poison for the other side.

The Founding Fathers of the United States kept religion out of the government because they were wise enough to know that god-based religions are a form of spiritual, intellectual and social dictatorship in exact opposition to democracy—and it was the dictatorship of religions that drove the first European colonists to North America.

And yet, despite the good intentions of the men who made up the power structure of American society discrimination of all kinds continued against females, non-Caucasians and especially black slaves and the original inhabitants of the Americas..

American Indians were regarded by most new white immigrants and their descendants as sub-human without rights, to be subjugated and confined or eliminated altogether. The latter "solution" was actively promoted on a state and local government level for some two centuries. Several American states as well as northern Mexican states bordering the U.S. paid bounties for the scalps of Indian men, women and children who had been hunted down and murdered.

Early Americans in one New England state also had small-pox infected blankets delivered to Indian tribes in their vicinity in ongoing attempts to exterminate them. So much for the ballyhooed "all men are created equal and have the right to life, liberty and the pursuit of happiness" concept of the Founding Fathers!

Incredibly, many of these discriminatory attitudes still exist in the psyche of Caucasian Americans, generally depending on what region of the country they were born and raised in, and the political goal of many is to make religious doctrines a key part of the American constitution.

Present-day demands that a political candidate be a Christian and prove his or her Christian beliefs is a primitive throwback to the days of the Catholic Inquisition. It should be obvious to any rational individual that claiming to be a Christian is not the best measure of a man or woman but that understanding is apparently beyond the ability of many people to comprehend.

The Voter Dilemma

To paraphrase some dry wit, political candidates, no matter how unsavory or incompetent they may be, can get elected to a public office if they can find enough fools to vote for them. And this pretty much sums up the electoral process in the United States today.

Voters often know very little if anything about the character, the competence or the background of most incumbent candidates, much less newcomers to politics. Instead of knowing enough to make wise choices voters more often than not go by the hype and crap spouted by the candidates and their handlers, and by their gender and their looks.

The figure and face of candidates are often the primary factors in their success or failure. Where candidates' names are on the ballot and the ethnic origin of their names influences many voters. Being able to talk endlessly and say almost nothing is another advantage.

Another of the worst elements of politics in many countries is the practice of sons and daughters replacing previous family generations, creating dynasties. This has long been a plague in Islamic countries.

The Plague of Money Politics

The only way to really reform the political system in the United States is to start by eliminating the money equation. Eliminating the hold that money politics now has on the country will require some drastic steps that only the public at large can initiate. Citizens must force their elected officials on every level of government to take the following simple steps:

1] Mandate by law that candidates cannot use paid advertisements in the news media or on signs, or have anyone else or any organization place paid advertisements on their behalf in or on any media.

2] Mandate by law that all citizens running for re-election, or election for the first time, write out in precise detail their biographical information and position on all issues that could be expected to come before them, and make their manifestos available to the public 90 days before the day of the election by releasing them to the print and electronic news media, and by printing and delivering them to voters in their districts and states.

3] Mandate by law that public campaigning by all candidates be limited to precisely 30 days before election day and that during this 30-day period they be prohibited from basing their campaigns on criticizing their opponents. If they are not willing to stand on their background and positions on the public interest they should not be running in the first place.

What the Public Has to Say

Among the many critiques of Congressional representatives and senators now on the Internet as pass-on messages, the following sums up the feelings of many Americans:

A. A maxim of two 6-year Senate terms.

B. A maxim of six 2-year House terms.

C. One 6-year Senate term and three 2-Year House terms.

D. Congressional members receive a salary while in office and no pension when they leave office.

E. Congressional members (past, present & future) participate in the Social Security program.

F. All funds in the Congressional retirement fund should be moved to the Social Security system immediately. All future funds should flow into the Social Security system, and Congressional members should participate with the American people.

G. Members of Congress should purchase retirement plans, just as other Americans do.

H. Congressional members should no longer have the right to vote themselves pay raises.

I. The current health care system for members of Congress should be eliminated, and they should participate in the same health care system as other Americans.

J. Members of Congress should be required to abide by the laws they impose on the American people.

K. All contracts with past and present members of Congressmen should be voided. The American people did not make these contracts with Congressional members. They made the contracts themselves.

L. Serving in Congress was not meant to be a career. The Founding Fathers envisioned citizen legislators, serving their term(s) then going home and going back to work.

A Common-Sense Manifesto

A board of independent ordinary citizens, business-people and scholars should draw up a simple common sense manifesto of specific incremental steps to take that over a period of years that are designed fix the problems now plaguing the infrastructure of the political system, the economic system, and the education system.

To implement this manifesto the American public would have to come to its senses, stop voting on party lines, and vote for independent candidates who pledge in writing to make the changes necessary, and then hold them strictly accountable if they are elected.

Politicians already in office should be required by voters to sign off on the manifesto. If they refuse to sign the manifesto they should be blacklisted in future elections—or better yet, recalled and booted out of office.

If such drastic steps are not taken there is no hope that basic improvements will be made in the governing process.

[11]
The Use of Sex & Violence in Business!

One of the most incredible results of the misunder-standing, misuse and abuse of human sexuality in the so-called Western world [which equates with the Christianized nations] has been the dramatic appear-ance and growth of sexual titillation industries since the advent of movies and television in the early 1900s.

This doesn't mean there was no sex-oriented media in earlier times. Drawings, paintings and even sculp-tures have long depicted men and women in the nude and in sex acts for their arousal effects.

In fact, in earlier times cultures in some Asian countries had enormous industries devoted to such things. Early Japan's famous 69-position sex charts are now collector's items worth large sums of money, and its annual sex festivals continue to attract hundreds of thousands of viewers. Sex-oriented sculptures of India, Cambodia and other Southeast Asian countries also continue to attract large numbers of tourists.

In the United States sex-oriented novels—most of them aimed at females—began to sell by the millions in the early 1900s. By the mid-1900s printed "fuck" comics and cartoons were big things in American high schools, furtively passed around by giggling girls and smirking boys in the classrooms and hallways. [Pop-eye was a popular star in the cartoons!]

But it was not until the hippie movement in the late 1950s and 1960s had influenced and liberated movie and television producers and magazine publishers that sexual titillation became one of the biggest industries in the country and one of the foundations of the whole economy.

As early as the 1970s hard-core porn films were available on television in hotel rooms, and despite some half-hearted attempts to stop the practice it continues—protected by the Freedom of Speech amendment attached to the American Constitution.

Visual and verbal pornography are now a mainstay of the movie and television industries. Even the broadcast news media has joined the sexual titillation crowd by selecting sexy female newscasters who are groomed fit to kill, wear short skirts, display a lot of naked leg and flirt with both guests and viewers.

As of this writing films showing both partial and complete nudity are now common fare on some television channels. Sexual intercourse depicting everything except the entry of the male penis into the female vagina is common.

Why Sex is used to Sell Everything!

Another of the incredible and conspicuous aspects of the failure of males in Jewish, Christian and Islamic societies to understand and deal humanely and effectively with the sexual nature of men and women is the fact that in the 20th century the display of female sexuality became the foundation of marketing in the United States, with several European and Hispanic countries following suit.

By 2005 even once sex-staid China has boarded the sex-marketing bandwagon, and it will be very interesting to watch that development both because the Chinese have a different cultural background regarding sex and because of the conservative influence that the Communist Party still has on the country.

The fact that it is primarily the use of *female* sexuality that primes the business pump in America and other Christianized countries is yet other outcome of the Jewish and Christian religions historically keeping women in the shadows and subservient to men—denying them the right of self-expression and making the subject of their sexuality both taboo and a subject of obsessive interest among males.

Islam has been and still is even more rigid and extreme in its efforts to keep women in virtual serfdom—a primitive practice that goes all the way back to caveman days and is just now beginning to show cracks because a tiny percentage of Islamic women have become educated enough, affluent enough and courageous to loosen the religious chains that have bound them since ancient times.

Hopefully, the influence of television and mobile communication devices will eventually override the hold that Islamic law has on females, allowing them to become fully realized human beings.

Another of the results of the religious-inspired laws requiring women to keep their bodies covered is that males in these countries have developed a fetish about female breasts. Surely never in the history of mankind has more been made about any part of the human body than what is now seen in the U.S., Mexico and other countries in regards to female tits.

Your might think that an American mother being arrested for breast-feeding her baby in public has to be the epitome of stupidity. But then along comes an Islamic cleric who announces in the Iranian media that women who engage in promiscuous behavior and whose dress reveals breast-cleavage and leg not only corrupts young men and leads to adultery but is also the cause of earthquakes.

This example of religious idiocy prompted Purdue University genetics and evolution student Jennifer Mc-Creight to create a 'boobquake" Facebook group as a joke…"to help fight supernatural thinking and the oppression of women just because they showed some cleavage."

In a matter of hours over 105,000 female *Facebook* users had volunteered to join the group, resulting in news media around the world picking up on the story. The site could become big and profitable—with many newcomers logging on because they think it is online pornography and they are going to see a lot of boobs.

What a marvelous story and what an amazing example of the power of the Internet to reveal the on-going idiocy and stupidity of primitive religious thinking and the susceptibility of the human mind to being programmed to believe anything.

Bras especially designed to reveal a lot of tit are big sellers. Plastic surgeons [mostly males] reacting to demand from hundreds of thousands of women have turned enlarging tits into another new industry.

But given the direction and the speed with which the breast fetish is driving "fashion" it seems safe to predict that totally bare breasts will eventually become so commonplace in public that the fetish will peter out.

What's Next? - The Male Penis?

Will the size and appearance of the erect male organ ever become a fetish among liberated females? I predicted that it would in *Brave New World of American Sex,* [written in the 1960s], and if it happens it will result in nationally televised contests and awards—resulting in fame and wealth for the extra-endowed men. [Basketball players would probably have to be banned from entering these contests because they would win most of them.]

Interestingly, centuries before Christianity became the primary religion in Rome sports-minded Romans staged penis contests in the gladiator stadium. The description of these popular coed events that especially caught my attention was the one about a man whose erect penis was so long he rested it on a wheel barrier as he proudly paraded it around the arena to rousing applause from the audience.

Such an event today would surely outdraw sports, and sponsors would be lined up by the hundreds.

The use of female sexuality to market products will no doubt continue until the sexuality of women is out in the open and no longer of obsessive interest to either males or females. That could be a long time coming because the influence of religions will remain strong for the foreseeable future.

The Entertainment Cesspool

Well before the end of the 20th century as much as seventy-five percent of all movie, television and mobile-device entertainment in the U.S. was based on sex, sleaze and violence.

The public display of female sexuality had also become one of the primary foundations of business in the United States, with several European and Hispanic countries soon following suit. It had spread to Japan by the 1970s; to China by 1990 and to South Korea by 2005.

The fact that it is primarily the use of female sexuality that primes the business pump in many countries is yet other outcome of the Jewish and Christian religions historically keeping women in the shadows and subservient to men, denying them the right of self-expression and making the subject of their sexuality both taboo and a subject of chronic obsessive interest among males.

In Muslim countries, however, Islamic customs and laws regarding female sexuality are still far too extreme and rigid to allow the use of sex as a basis for business or entertainment. Even minor infractions of these rules result in serious punishment. Conspicuous infractions can lead to death.

In pre-Americanized Japan, men and women bathed together in large public bathhouses as a normal, natural thing, and women's breasts were not considered erotic—the back of the neck exposed by the kimono was *the* erotic zone! But since the 1960s breasts have also become a big thing in Japan, as the

Japanese became more and more under the influence of sleazy American culture.

Interestingly, promoting prurient interest in female breasts had gone so far by the turn of the century that marketers in the fashion industry had begun to zero in on female butts as the new thing. Some of the commercials focusing on the butts of shapely females are more sexually arousing than the cleavage and breast ads because female butts are far more directly associated with actual sexual intercourse than mammary glands.

By 2011 TV commercials had begun focusing on the butts of men wearing tight blue jeans in yet another marketing gambit with a powerful sexual message.

Porn and Prostitution

The obsession with sex that is characteristic of people who have been programmed by anti-sex religions has resulted in the growth of pornography from a minor business to one of the world's largest and most profitable enterprises. First fueled by the advent of sex-based movies and television in the mid-1900s, pornography went viral virtually overnight when the Internet came along.

Visual and verbal pornography are now a mainstay of the movie and television industries. Google porn sites and porn videos on the Internet and the figure that comes up is well above forty million. Huge numbers of porn videos are advertised as free. Many porn producing companies have large numbers of members who pay a reduced fee for each new release.

In addition to the huge personal, individual market for hard-core pornographic films delivered on television and other electronic devices the market for packaged porno DVDs is huge and growing.

As incredible as it seems on the surface, the right to produce, distribute and sell pornography is protected by the "Freedom of Speech" provision in the American Bill of Rights…a right repeatedly reaffirmed by the Supreme Court of the United States and buttressed by an army of lawyers paid by pornographers.

As far back as the mid-1970s *Hustler* magazine publisher Larry Flynt had an attorney on a $15,000 a month retainer to fight off lawsuits if and when they occurred. This monthly expense was probably next only to the cost of printing the magazine but it was pocket change to the publisher. Despite the unsavory media-created reputation Flynt had as a smut peddler, he had goals that were more admirable than those claimed by many religions. His aim was to force people to be honest and aboveboard about their prejudices and sex obsessions, face them, and overcome them. He knew his approach was shocking to the average person. He also knew absolutely that it would make him immensely rich, but he was honest about it.

Again, the incredible market for porn was not created by the pornographers. It was created by the religious teachings that sexual behavior outside of marriage and not for the purpose of procreation is a sin against a vengeful God and those guilty of ignoring these teachings would go to Hell.

To prevent men from being aroused and seduced by females the religions mandated that women keep their bodies covered and not engage in any kind of licentious behavior. In some societies the sanctions to enforce these mandates included death—a sick male response still in force in some Islamic communities.

The very successful efforts of religions to deny, ignore and subvert both male and female sexuality naturally resulted in males becoming pathologically obsessive about female sexuality.

Male pornographers are not the only ones who take advantage of this cultural aberration. Since women are naturally smarter than men, some who are liberated have taken advantage of the male obsession with female sexuality to create their own porn sites.

Porn Tycoons & Religions!

People who are profiting from pornography—some of whom have become billionaires—should bow down several times a day to the God-based religions—Judaism, Christianity and Islam—that have misunderstood and abused human sexuality since their inception, resulting in much of humanity becoming obsessed with sex, with sexual genitalia…with everything that has to do with sex.

Despite claims to the contrary, it is sex that runs the world, not love. And as long as the sexual nature of human beings is denied, ignored and suppressed, and people are punished for breaking the religious taboos designed to dramatically limit sexual expression, the obsession is not going to go away.

In other words, the profit morality will continue to prevail…at the expense of the religious elements that in fact are rational and humane but cannot compete with the power of the sexual nature of humanity.

As said, even the broadcast news media has joined the sexual titillation crowd by selecting sexy female newscasters who are groomed fit to kill, wear short skirts revealing a lot of leg, and flirt with both guests and viewers.

The Traditional Sex Trade

The traditional sex trade itself is, of course, one of the world's largest and most enduring industries, even though it continuously inflicts immeasurable suffering on millions of young girls and women.

Not surprisingly, the business of sex has long been fodder for the modern-day news media, which periodically covers it like any other news category but never gets down to the nitty-gritty of why the industry continues to flourish on such a massive scale.

Selling and buying sex also periodically gets the attention of politicians and religious leaders who routinely decry its presence, but they too ignore the underlying reasons for its existence. And as is well known, many of them participate in the action themselves, although they try to keep it secret.

You might think that there is some kind of conspiracy going on—a worldwide conspiracy that both allows and protects the sex industry from serious interference by anyone or any organization. And you would be right.

The conspiracy is as ancient as the industry itself, and is an outgrowth of the natural sexual instincts of males to have sexual relations with females on a regular basis—and to have sexual access to more than one female whenever possible.

As noted earlier, this predatory sexual nature of males is a built-in characteristic that is a fundamental part of the survival instinct of all organic life forms. In some human males this drive can be so powerful it prevents them from thinking and behaving rationally, and when it is denied and/or repressed bad things can happen.

In males sexual energy builds up like a battery being charged. When the energy in the "sex battery" of males is not dispelled by having intercourse (or masturbating) it begins to have a negative impact on them. Their thinking and their behavior changes, and those with more powerful sex drives often resort to some kind and degree of violence to obtain sexual release.

Females are also genetically imbued with a survival instinct and are driven to attract males to impregnate them, but from the first days of the human species they were under the control of males who were superior in size and strength, and they were subject to being severely punished if not killed if they did not ac-commodate males who approached them.

As the human species advanced intellectually and began to form larger and larger groups it gradually became customary in most societies for the male rulers and their male-priest allies to establish rules that limit-ed most men to one wife at a time, or prescribed the maximum number of wives they could have—a move-ment that totally ignored the sexual nature of most males and all females.

As is also well known, in many societies these limi-tations did not apply to the rulers and top officials, re-sulting in concubine and mistress-keeping become

common among the ruling elite and the wealthy min-
ority who were invariable aligned with the political
and religious leaders.

The Bible notes that the famous King Solomon—
the leader of a relatively small Jewish tribe—had 700
wives and 300 concubines. This sounds like a far-out
exaggeration meant to burnish Solomon's manly
image, but such numbers are a matter of historical
record in a number of cultures.

But whatever the society and whatever social system it had, a large number of men always ended up
without the opportunity for regular sexual release.
And, of course, many who had wives simply gave in to
the urge to have extra-marital sex. These factors combined with the material and security needs of many
females and their families led to the early development of sex as a trade.

In some cultures religious leaders recognized and
accepted the true nature of men, and created a system
in which men, married or single, could have sex with
female priests and acolytes. [Interestingly, Hawaiians
had separate "sex houses" for royalty and for commoners that featured a variety of sex games. One game
for commoners consisted of bowling for sex—rolling a
wobbly coconut across a floor toward a lineup of
females to select a partner for the night... surely hoping
it would go to one that was attractive.*

---

*This custom was banned by American missionaries when
they arrived in Hawaii only a few years after the islands
were discovered by English seafaring explorer James Cook
in 1778. If Hawaii ever runs short of tourists all it would
have to do is restart the bowling-for-sex game.

Obviously, political, social and religious leaders have never resolved the sexual nature of males or females, which explains why the sex trade has survived into modern times. In short, it serves the purpose and needs of many males, and, in a perverse way, some females.

As is well known, law enforcement agencies in the U.S. periodically attempt to keep the sex trade behind closed doors, typically targeting females instead of males, even though the trade caters almost exclusively to males and would not exist if there was no demand.

As the cultural restraints against extra-marital sex and consensual sex among singles weaken, the need for commercial sex may diminish, but it will not go away in the foreseeable future; not as long as so many men need—or think they need—the services the trade provides.

The only way that the sex trade could be dramatically and quickly reduced in size would be mandatory government-enforced use of chemicals to block the natural sex drive of men. That will not happen as long as males are in control.

The "natural solution" that seems to be developing is a simple sexual free-for-all situation that is culturally approved as long as it is consensual.

This is an area of human behavior that the education system must eventually address in a rational, honest and humane way, beginning with middle school students, because parents cannot or will not do it.

The Violence Syndrome In Popular Culture

In the 1960s the American movie industry began to use brutality and extreme depictions of violence to increase the popularity and profitability of its films. In no time, the surefire fix for a successful movie was violence and sex, and that combination transitioned into video games for children.

From the 1980s on all Americans who viewed and or listened to public entertainment were fed a diet of violence, with the producers and sellers insisting that exposure to such fare did not influence the behavior of either adults or children, and cloaking themselves in the "Freedom of Speech" provision of the Constitution to justify their actions.

The third factor in the growth of the entertainment industries from the 1960s on was the introduction of verbal sleaze—of language that was designed to shock. By the first decade of the 21st century, "fuck you," "fucking this" and "fucking that" had become a conspicuous part of the dialogue of both male and female entertainers...with some newscasters beginning to use such terms as "the F word," in a move in the same direction.

Not surprisingly, the news media were major partners in the spread of entertainment based on violence, sex and sleaze—glaring evidence that even the most upright appearing people will lower themselves to dealing in smut to continue making a profit.

Entertainers & Drugs

The use of so-called recreational and medicinal drugs in the United States is a threat to the nation. The fact that it has been allowed to develop to this point is a national disgrace and should get money-oriented businesses, parents, teachers, educators and elected officials who are responsible for letting it happen indicted as accessories to a crime.

The rampant use of recreational drugs in the United States took off in the late 1950s and early 1960s, first promoted by so-called Hippies, "rock" musicians and counter-culture news media. It quickly spread to other entertainers, particularly to young people in the movie and television industries, and finally to students all the way down to the 7th and 8th grade levels of elementary schools.

Well before the end of the 20th century recreational drug use in the United States had become a multi-billion dollar a year industry, involved hundreds of thousands of people, and was a national tragedy that business and political communities could not resolve. The problem has continued to grow simply because of the money-morality and corruption that now pervades American culture.

Not surprisingly, substance abuse has generally been highest among young males in the lowest income and educational brackets—Blacks and Hispanics—but millions of Whites from middle and upper class families have also given in to the seductive power of getting high on drugs, primarily because of the influence of the entertainment industries.

The New Drug Lords

Major pharmaceutical companies are big players in this American tragedy, spending billions of dollars a year on television, in print media and on the Internet hyping drugs they claim will cure all of the ailments, complaints and problems that people have—from bad complexions, hair loss, obesity and sexual dysfunctions to getting old—creating an environment in which taking drugs is a natural and necessary part of life.

The world's largest and most dangerous drug lords are not Mexican or Columbian. They are American; they are the heads of the huge drug companies and their doctor distributors who are all licensed to engage in the drug trade. George Orwell's frightening novel *1984*, in which the government conspired to get the whole country addicted to drugs got it right.

Given the history of the United States it now seems inevitable that the only action the government can and eventually will take is to make the use of marijuana—the most commonly used illegal drug—legal and tax it, the way it did to alcohol and tobacco when it lost the ability to control these substances—both of which are more harmful and more destructive than pot.

Blame for this incredible situation also falls on parents, educators and politicians—some of whom were part of the problem because they were among the pot-smoking generations. Far too many of them still today stand by and watch silently as the entertainment media aimed at the young hype the use of drugs among handsome, well-to-do and successful people in attractive sensually oriented settings.

When the Mexican government began giving serious consideration to legalizing pot in 2010 as the only way of getting the drug-related murders, bribery of government officials and law enforcement members under control, the president of Mexico made the obvious point that unless the United States—the largest market for the drug—also made pot legal, making it legal in Mexico would not work.

Eskimo:
"If I did not know about God and sin,
would I go to hell?"

Priest:
"No! Not if you didn't know."

Eskimo:
"Then why did you tell me?"

—Annie Dillard—

[12]
The Advertising Conspiracy

Product, service and entertainment advertising has become a cancer eating away at the physical, mental and spiritual health of mankind—all in the name of profit.

The American advertising industry has long been looked upon as one of the bulwarks of both the democratic and the capitalistic systems that have defined the United States since the early 1800s. It goes without saying that both of these systems have made extraordinary contributions to the wealth and welfare of Americans, but there have always been elements in these systems that were destructive and harmful, and these insidious elements have grown with time.

In earlier times advertising was important in bringing the existence and benefits of products and services to the attention of as many people as possible so they would know where to buy them if they needed them. From around the 1950s and 60s the manufacturing and service industries became so competitive that the role of advertising gradually switched to beating out the competition, to inducing people to buy more than what they needed, and to buying things they didn't need...in other words attempting to ensure that the companies not only survived but made a profit above and beyond what the market would normally provide them.

One of the most negative aspects of advertising today is that a great deal of it is aimed at children and teenagers, and is insidiously clever, subversive and harmful.

The advertising industry's sophisticated selling of sugar-laden cereals and other foods to children sets them up for obesity and a variety of other health problems. Glamorizing alcoholic drinks to teens and adults and getting millions of people habituated to drugs they don't need—some of which have serious side effects—costs Americans billions of dollars annually.

Advertising aimed at children and teens ignores commonsense and undercuts the little parental control remaining by inducing the young to eat and drink things that are bad for their health and will adversely affect the rest of their lives. It encourages other behavior that results in further degrading cultures that are already in the gutter.

The causes of this phenomenon are well known but they are so deeply entrenched in the profit-oriented culture that they cannot be eradicated without a mass rebellion by individual consumers that is not going to happen in the foreseeable future..

But if an effort to eliminate this disease is not made—by parents and teachers—the negative impact on the welfare of the young will continue to grow, further degrading the culture.

There are equally harmful areas of advertising aimed at adults that are contributing to the degeneration of the culture in general—from the education problem to the degradation of the Earth's environment.

The Excess-Consumption Disease

By the end of the 20th century aggressive profit-driven advertising had created an excess-consumption syndrome that prevailed throughout the American economy and had begun spreading throughout the economies of other industrialized nations. It has now reached the point that it has destroyed much of the rational thought process, and controls much of the mindset and behavior of a growing percentage of the Earth's population.

There would appear to be no remedy for this insidious virus other than for parents, teachers and administrators who recognize the dangers inherent in this situation to slowly but steadily introduce into the basic education of children a new value system based on real, actual, rational needs that would eventually result in the excess-consumption syndrome disappearing in conjunction with a balanced economic system.

It is not going to disappear any time soon but by 2010 there was a glimmer of hope. The news media had begun reporting on the appearance of a small movement among the economically depressed population to downgrade their consumption habits and expectations—not as a deliberate choice, however, but because of the economic situation.

Some of these people were reported as saying that having and consuming less freed them from harmful habits and made them happier than they were before—both common sense and very old wisdom.

The Incredible Obesity Epidemic

Another cultural failure resulting from a combination of the power of food manufacturers, their advertising agencies, and the willful stupidity of parents in particular and adults in general is the epidemic of obesity in the United States.

The sight of huge numbers of men and women who weigh from 300 to 500 pounds or more waddling around like giant over-inflated character balloons is grotesque to say the least.

The number of children and adults who are obese is a national disgrace and should be a national scandal. But there has been a conspiracy among food producers, food outlets, their advertizing agencies and the medical fraternity to both justify this incredible situation and to blame the individuals for overeating.

Some medical experts are on record as saying that obesity is not the fault of every obese person, claiming that it is genetic, which actually appears to be partly true, since fat mothers give birth to unusually large babies who appear to inherit a propensity to become obese.

This incredible malady has resulted from both the willful stupidity of parents and people in general and the business obsession with making profits no matter what the cost to the public. The only permanent cure is education over a period of a generation or more.

That is happening but very slowly because deeply ingrained habits are extremely difficult to break, the power of advertising, and human failings.

A New Universal Strategy

Of course, it goes without saying that a universal strategic plan is needed to address all of the economic needs of all countries on an equitable basis. However, this is a concept that brings into play all of the ancient and primitive characteristics of human beings—tribalism, territorialism, religious differences, races and colors, along with past history, the present situation, territorial size, population, location, and so on.

This means it will not be resolved in the foreseeable future by plan and by action because some or all of the larger more powerful nations will put their priorities high on the list if not first. This means the evolution from competition to cooperation with have to come about in slow incremental steps.

It might not come about at all if there is not a concerted effort among the large and powerful nations to incorporate the concept of a shared world into their education systems, to wean their populations off of the ancient prejudices, the old animosities and the selfish instincts.

I like your Christ.
I do not like your Christians.
Your Christians are so unlike your Christ.

—*Mohandas Gandhi*—

[13]
The News Media Virus

Adapting to the New Profit Morality

Like all other areas of the American economy the mantra and imperative of the news media has always been to make a profit. But with the advent of the Internet making it possible for virtually anyone to become a news source the collapse of news media standards in the pursuit of profit was inevitable.

The negative influence of today's news media is incredible. It is blatantly obvious and getting worse by the day. It adversely affects virtually every area of life—socially, economically, politically and spiritually—and despite all of the hemming and hawing by people who recognize its destructive influence, it continues to make a mockery of common sense, rationality and any pretense of positive morality.

Much of this morass derives from the misuse of the Constitutional provision regarding freedom of speech to advance the fortunes of individuals; to make money in total disregard for the damage it causes.

One aspect of the degradation of American culture that was stoked by the so-called Hippie Movement in the 1960s was the practice among both young men and women to get tattoos to demonstrate their rebellion against Establishment values and customs.

This rebellion was primarily voiced and advanced by songs and music that broke all of the old taboos against vulgar behavior and dress—something that appealed directly to the very young on a subconscious level.

Profit-oriented movie and television producers joined this rebellion and began to promote the same ideas and behavior that had grown out of the Hippie Movement—outlandish fashions, female nudity, unrestricted sexual activity, tattooed anti-heroes and gratuitous violence…all of which are now as American as apple pie.

Just one small part of this rebellion was the growing incidence of tattoos among young girls after the Hippies had faded into the background—something that just a generation earlier would have been unthinkable. By the first decade of the 21st century the news media had begun to cooperate with entrepreneurial tattoo artists to promote tattoos as an "in" thing to do, with national tattoo organizations and annual "tattoo festivals."

This tattoo phenomenon can be blamed on the failure of parents and educators to instill sensible values and common sense into the mindset of the young—not to mention that copious body decorations have historically been associated with small tribes of people still on the savage level who used it as a tribal marker, and in more modern times with biker gangs, low ranking sailors, marines and soldiers.

And here too the news media is at fault for treating the practice as a stylish thing to do.

The Black Hole of Competition

A huge portion of the daily, weekly and monthly print news media in the United States abrogated any pretense of standing for and upholding a rational level of moral behavior when their existence was threatened by competition from broadcast and online news media as well as other print media. They lowered their standards or they died.

This corruption is especially glaring and conspicuous in the manner in which these publications report on and hype the entertainment industries that specialize in content based on soft and hard pornography, violence and sleazy behavior in general—much of which is aimed at young people, including children.

Very good writers in publications that once stood for honesty and integrity now utilize their skills to cleverly hawk the movies, television shows, video games and books that in another time and another place would be banned.

Public relations professionals hired by companies and individuals, along with gossip columnists published by newspapers and magazines, are also guilty of using their well-honed talents to promote ill-advised products and agendas by encasing them in an aura of integrity, value and glamour.

Comic strips in newspapers and comedians on television have become social commentators with agendas of their own, subtly making anti-social and anti-human behavior sound like okay fun. Film makers inject far out political agendas into movies promoted as entertainment.

There are still honest and forthright journalists and publications in the news media field, but their numbers are dwindling and the cacophony erupting from their anything-that-will-sell competitors drowns most of them out.

The primary force in the motivation and goals of most of America's professional news media today is simply to get as much of the spoils of war as they can. Some publications have simply eliminated any restraints or standards on what they publish.

The Insidious Enemy Within

The widespread disappearance of integrity among members of the news media of America has resulted in many of these journalists, commentators and columnists becoming the equivalent of war-time 5th Columns—spies and saboteurs—whose misinformation and slanted news has negative and destructive effects on the country at large.

Unlike spies and saboteurs, however, most of these individuals and enterprises do not work under cover. They are out in public with as big a bang as possible, and the more notice they get and the more they are criticized, the more they like it because that attracts larger audiences and they get paid more by the advertisers who sponsor them.

The insidious power of these elements in the press is virtually unbounded. They can and do control the attitudes and behavior of millions of people.

In the present contexts of American culture any hope of returning integrity and responsibility to the news media is not possible. It will continue as long as it is both supported and driven by the overall culture of the country. It is a symptom of the obsession to make money.

[14]
The Age of Robots
&
Technology as God!

Sophisticated robotic devices were standard in many manufacturing operations by the 1980s. The use of such devices in all areas of manufacturing, warehousing and distribution has continued to grow, and by 2010 in Japan and elsewhere humanized robots were in use in many service industries.

It takes no great intellect to realize that robotic devices and humanized robots are going to continue replacing a significant proportion of all manual labor tasks as well as many of the tasks in virtually all other fields of endeavor, including health care and surgery, within this century.

Coming to terms with this new world will be one of the most fundamental cultural and industrial challenges mankind has ever faced.

The future of robotic devices in the health care industry was abundantly clear by 2011 when over one thousand American hospitals were using the da Vinci robot to perform prostate cancer removal and other delicate operations…and the use of the da Vinci robot alone was growing worldwide.

Pioneered and promoted by India-born Dr. Mani Menon, director of the Vattikuti Urology Institute at Henry Ford, the da Vinci robot is a harbinger of things to come.

The integration of high-tech devices into education systems in the U.S. was also well underway by the end of the first decade of the 21st century, and their number and sophistication will continue to increase with each passing year. The question is: how far will they go in replacing live teachers.

The programming of robots to have the most desirable qualities of human beings has advanced so rapidly that some are already smarter than humans and capable of interacting with humans on a sophisticated level.

Fans of the prescient television and film series *STAR TREK, The Next Generation* [which began in 1987] have only to consider the robot *Lt. Commander Data* to clearly see where robotics are going. *Data* is smarter, stronger and faster than any human being could ever be, never needs rest, never needs sleep, can absorb huge amounts of new information in milliseconds, never forgets anything, and doesn't deteriorate with age.

By 2010 in Japan robots were already being used as assistant nurses, assistant doctors, maids, tour guides, information specialists, product spokesmen, guards, and more. There is virtually no end to what robots can be programmed to do now, and with each passing year they will be able to do more and do it better.

The question is: how will human beings deal with future *Datas*. Will they all be programmed to be tolerant and kind and protective of human beings and do only good things?

Given the history of humanity the answer to this question is not necessarily "Yes." It is very likely that some of the engineers who create or obtain and program the first *Datas* will be influenced by their culture, their race, their tribal affiliations, their religions and so on—a frightening thought.

Robots have been used as weapons of war since the early 21st century, and long before they approach the sophistication and abilities of Lt. Commander Data they will make up most of the armed forces.

As far back as 2006 writer Bill Christensen noted that Japan's Ministry of Economy, Trade and Industry was working on a new set of safety guidelines for next-generation robots. Their set of regulations constituted the first attempt at a formal version of the *Laws of Robotics*, conceived by the science-fiction writer Isaac Asimov in 1940, or at least the portion that states that humans shall not be harmed by robots.

The first law of robotics as set forth by Asimov states: *A robot may not injure a human being, or, through inaction, allow a human being to come to harm.*

Of course, the greatest danger that might come from highly intelligent robots—also already suggested by science-fiction movies—is that they would become self-aware and decide to make humans their servants—or worse.

The only hope for humanity is that the superior intelligence of robots—and no human history baggage in their brain chips—would result in them becoming gods instead of devils.

One of Japan's top robotics experts, Dr. Hiroshi Ishiguro, who designed and built a robot based on his appearance as well as his mindset and behavior says that human-like robots are mirrors that reflects human beings and should be treated as such—a very sobering thought.

In the meantime, and on a brighter side, one of the most obvious uses of smart robots at this time in history is as teachers. Just image: no pay; no time off; no emotional meltdowns; no incompetence; no unions!

Technology as God!

Given all the negative influences in the cultures of the world the only salvation for humanity may be technology—which by itself is rapidly changing all of the world's cultures.

In the long run, even without forward thinking and forward-acting leaders, the world's cultures will become more and more rational, and more and more democratic because of the universal and objective, influence of technology.

But given the fact that primitive religions and authoritarian political forms still have at least a partial death-grip on the majority of mankind, these transformations could take generations because educators and political leaders will not take the heroic steps necessary to change today's morality and today's policies...even if they *want* it to happen!

And, of course, there are many leaders who are dead-set against freedom and against a humane morality for the people they rule over.

As a result, many people may continue to be oppressed and prevented from achieving their full potential for generations to come...unless these changes are aggressively promoted by huge numbers of people blogging the world's bureaucrats and leaders in business, in politics and in religions with exposure, criticism and advice! And even more importantly, by simply refusing to go along with stupid, insane policies and the people who promote them!

Of course, the majority of people everywhere are sickened by the world's cultural failures. But survival, power and profit-making...not moral behavior...are the overwhelming goals of most leaders in politics and business. And as already said, there is no way that the weak, divided and often irrational spiritual-based moralities of today are going to change that!

We therefore need to teach and follow a philosophy of living and working that is based on common sense, on the fragile nature of the Earth, on the real physical, emotional, intellectual, spiritual and philosophical needs of human beings.

Of course, there are people already espousing these philosophies but with so little impact that contemplating the future is frightening. Despite the misuse and abuse of the Internet by hate mongers, pornographers and radical religious zealots, this new technology also makes it possible for the average person to make his or her voice heard on a large scale for the first time in the history of mankind.

Ordinary people can now vote and express themselves online at any time on very important issues of the day! If enough rational and morally enlightened people will bring more and more pressure against leaders in every field to force them to give up their self-serving ways—or force them out of positions of authority and let a new breed of people have a go at it—the ancient religious promise of peace on Earth might be achieved.

Two of the more obvious things that we in the United States are now talking about—and could do if we had the will—is to reintroduce discipline and a reality-based future-oriented curriculum into the educational system, and to boycott purveyors of obscene, immoral and harmful ideas and behavior instead of rewarding them with fame and great wealth.

Just as obviously, the First Amendment of the Constitution should be amended to prohibit its abuse by the so-called entertainment industries—and the so-called news media as well. In addition to being morally inexcusable, the present system is socially insane.

One of the fundamental imperatives in bringing humanity into the new world of the 21st century within a universal culture is the need for a higher level of wisdom combined with better training systems that are integrated into the culture. This wisdom has existed for millennia and there have been some examples of education and training systems that created outstanding people.

However, humans have screwed up and misused far simpler technology than what is now appearing in the world of robotics, which pales with what will appear just in the next few decades. Without a dramatic overhaul of world cultures, based on a 21st century education system, technology will no doubt continue to be both God and Satan.

Cultural Revolution Underway

The male-dominated business, political and religious institutions that have traditionally molded and controlled the mindset and behavior of people are losing their hold on humanity because of cultural changes and technology that is exposing their abuse and misuse of power to the public at large, making it possible for ordinary people to make their own decisions.

Television, with all of its good and bad elements, has become the new family, the new church, and the new school room of humanity. The stupidity, the perfidy, and the inhumanity that is shown in unending broadcasts from around the world is so shocking that the innate goodness in most of humanity that has long been ignored, oppressed and impotent—except in case of revolutions brought on by mass rebellions—is finally beginning to make itself felt through nonviolent means.

If a man would follow, today, the
teachings of the Old Testament,
he would be a criminal.
If he would follow strictly the
teachings of the New Testament,
he would be insane.

—*Robert Green Ingersol*—

Technology as God *and* Satan!

Given all the negative influences in today's cultures, the only salvation for humanity may be the positive influence of technology—which by itself is already rapidly changing all of the world's cultures. In the long run, even without courageous forward thinking and forward-acting leaders, the world's cultures will become more and more rational, and more and more democratic because of the incomparable ability of technology to inform, to educate, to encourage critical thinking and to change the behavior of people—and especially to influence people to demand their natural rights to be free and secure.

But given the fact that primitive religions and authoritarian political forms still have a death-grip on the majority of mankind, these transformations could take generations—time the Earth does not have—because leaders will not or cannot take the heroic steps necessary to change today's morality and today's policies even if they *want* these things to happen!

The Free Speech Bucket of Worms

Many Americans believe freedom of speech is guaranteed by the Constitution and gives people the right to say or write almost anything, no matter how gross or false it might be.

But constitutional authority Robert Greenslade says that is not so. He says the sole purpose of the Bill of Rights was to add restraints to the powers of the federal government, and that the "rights" should be called the "Bill of Prohibitions" instead of the Bill of Rights.

The original purpose of the "Rights," Greenslade adds, was to reserve these rights to individuals as the "natural rights" of mankind rather than leave them in the hands of politicians.

As a result, the rights inherent in the individual amendments did not take into account the possibility that they could and might be abused.

[15]

Challenges Facing Mankind!

To recap, it is patently obvious male-created religious doctrines designed to control the sexual behavior of both males and females have had unforeseen results that made the lives of both men and women a travesty of their nature.

Another fallout from the misunderstanding and misuse of human sexuality is the declining custom of marriage and the increase in children born out of wedlock...both of which have a powerful, negative effect on the stability of societies and the quality of life.

By the turn of the century the economic impact of single parent families among minorities and especially illegal immigrants.—all of whom qualified for government handouts of cash, rebates and food stamps—had become one of the largest tax burdens in the U.S.

The sexual revolution that now encompasses much of humanity—again caused by the mostly well-intentioned attempts of religious doctrines to limit sexual behavior and channel it into narrow confines—is still in its early stages. Where and how far it will go remains to be seen but it cannot be allowed to run the course set for it by the present profit-at-any-cost based morality.

Of course, striving to transform the many cultures of the world and create a global Earth Culture is a challenge of epic proportions. In addition to the religious obstacles there is the automobile industry, the oil industry and the use of sex as the foundation of the advertising, marketing and entertainment industries—all of which fly in the face of common sense.

The profits involved in the automobile and oil industries alone virtually rule the world, and in today's world profit comes before morality, before sanity, and especially before the future! It goes without saying that these two industries are not going to change their stripes anytime soon! They will surely milk the oil and automobile cows as long as it is profitable—or at least until they have managed to come up with other ways of producing energy and transportation modes that allow them to continue to control much of the economies of the world.

The blatant, gross use of sex in business is another of the most negative legacies of the religious distortion and repression of the sexual impulse. Even once straight-laced Asian countries have picked up on the American way of using sex to sell. This misuse and abuse of human sexuality is also not going to go away until we manage to create a new ethic for sexual behavior that is rational, satisfying and doable.

As already noted, we also need to obliterate the religious doctrines that continue to contribute to unsustainable population growth. Neither planet Earth nor "God" needs more people, and the Church-based obsession that "He" does is another kind of pathological insanity!

Furthermore, the religious-economic-political concept that prosperity and the quality of life are based on a continuously growing population is not only outdated, it is one of the primary factors in the poverty that plagues over half of the population of the Earth, including millions of people in the most prosperous nations.

Over-population is also one of the primary sources of much of the violence that afflicts so much of mankind. In fact, the world needs some kind of parental code of ethics that people be required to agree to before they have children—in or outside of wedlock. To start with, courses in parenting responsibilities and skills should be made a mandatory part of the education of the young.

The political, economic and social policies of promoting growth and more growth for political and religious power must be eliminated from the human mindset. Economic growth should first of all be designed to raise the level of the living standard of all people on Earth to a comfortable level while ensuring that it is sustainable both during the process and afterward.

All of the prevailing reasons why men go to war—religion, the hunger for political power, the obsession with wealth, territorial ambitions, oppressive government regimes—should be eliminated by a coordinated universal effort that now seems to be so far beyond the ability of mankind that it is not even a dream. But that is exactly what at least ninety-five percent of the people on Earth want! So why can't it be done?

It *can* be done but it will not be done until religious and political leaders are no longer in the dark ages where ignorance, irrationality and inhuman behavior are the norm—the norm for them; not for the people at large.

One factor that raised the living standard of people in China and India—two countries that represent two-thirds of humanity—was work out-sourcing from the United States, Japan, South Korea and other developed countries, a phenomena that began with Japan in the 1950s and from there spread to Hong Kong, Korea, Taiwan and Singapore.

As controversial and as painful to some as this phenomenon was, it nevertheless was the most efficient and practical means of quickly achieving more economic parity between nations.

The more affluent developing countries become, the more they contribute to the economies of the countries out-sourcing to them, the more stable their governments, and the more likely they are to cherish and work for peace and prosperity.

Of course, there are many other things that should be done. And despite all of the gloom and doom scenarios facing humanity today the great majority of people on this endangered planet are good-hearted, well-behaved and hardworking, and want only to live peaceful, comfortable, secure lives.

The evil doers—leaders and their henchmen who are actually well-known to the world—number only in the thousands. If the world could somehow get rid of them and prevent others from taking their place the

Earth could become a sane, safe habitat for humanity in a very short period of time.

The material quality of life is primarily determined by knowing what to do and having the political and religious freedom to do it. This makes it imperative that all people be freed from the destructive religious, political and economic shackles of the past.

Solving the Sex Problem

Everywhere you look there are powerful images and signs of the dysfunction of cultures—much of which could be eliminated by the creation of a practical solution for the sexual needs of males and females beginning at the age of puberty.

One way that would resolve or reduce the problem of providing males and females with sexual partners when they need or want them would be to formally and legally allow unattached men and women to provide sexual services to those who need or want them on a commercial basis.

Licenses could be issued to men and women who are not married and above the age of consent, to divorcees, and to widows and to widowers—a solution that would dramatically reduce the buildup of sexual energy in both males and females, and provide gainful employment for millions of people.

What a boon to the service industry this would be! And just image the income from licensing fees... which could quickly reach the level of government income from tobacco, alcohol and other drugs.

Sexual potency is at its peak in both males and females from the age of puberty to around the mid-20s, and expecting and sometimes forcing them to refrain from sexual intercourse until they get married is both irrational and harmful in many ways.

The solution to this real problem is simply to formally and officially allow young unmarried males and females to have intimate relationships as soon as they are old enough to take the responsibility necessary for them to avoid pregnancies and venereal diseases.

These practices would eliminate most of the sexual stress that afflicts younger unmarried males and females; it would help prevent these same people from growing up to have a variety of harmful sexual hangups; it would also eliminate most of the obsession with sexual titillation that now passes as entertainment... and it could help teens become more responsible adults in their sexual relationships.

The facts are, of course, that young males and females in some countries, including the United States, are already creating this new paradigm on their own, with or without the approval of their parents, other adults and institutions of whatever kind.

Still another suggestion is that married men and women could agree to be free to have civilized, harmonious affairs with other partners without negative effect on their marriage—something that would no doubt roil the "me-only" ego of many males. But the positive benefits of this customs could be miraculous. Men who didn't want to lose their wives would be better husbands. Women who didn't want to lose their husbands would be better wives.

Surprising to some, perhaps, this trend is also well underway. Surveys show that around one-third of American married men and women over the age of 40 have had extra-marital affairs, and a larger percentage think it is a good idea.

Of course, people who did not have spouses should be free to have mutually consensual intimate relationships with anyone of their choice—also already a growing reality in the U.S. and elsewhere.

If these practices were followed, there would be far less sexual frustration among both men and women, the tendency for male violence would be dramatically reduced, and the world would be a saner, happier place.

The time is long past when religions and other institutions that don't work in the first place should be eliminated as the controllers of the sexual behavior of human beings. There is nothing sacred or profane about sex. It is simply the way life works, and when this natural process is denied or perverted problems are inevitable.

A man sooner or later discovers
that he is the master-gardener of his soul,
the director of his life.

—*James Allen*—

[16]
The Need for a New Cultural Paradigm!

Mankind is now faced with new challenges spawned by the stupidity and idiocy of traditional cultures. In the U.S. and elsewhere this has led to the use of technology to create new cultures that in some respects are worse than the old ones.

It goes without saying that to truly meet the physical, emotional, intellectual and spiritual needs of mankind the world needs a new, global, cultural paradigm that "fits" and enhances the lives of everybody in all societies.

But are there principles and policies that would ensure high standards of ethical behavior and would work on a worldwide basis? There are, but to create and implement this new paradigm would mean discarding all of the institutionalized and ritualized one-God cult religions. [The only difference between these three cults and notorious *little* cults is that these three are very big and very powerful, and can ignore and squash criticism].

It is, of course, a fact that some of the social tenets of Judaism and Christianity are responsible for much of the humane morality that has managed to survive in the United States and other Western countries. But even the most casual glance at the level of morality in so-called Christianized societies reveals that corrupttion and immoralities of all kinds are thriving as never before.

Christianity now presents itself as humane and nurturing. But it is still off-base in many of its teachings—and has never been and is not now capable of instilling a desirable standard of morality even in "Christianized" countries, much less universally.

Islam is even worse in many respects. It remains caught in a time warp, with many of the same irrational and barbarous tenets that were the bedrock of Christianity for many centuries—the same Christianity that was responsible for the crusades against Muslims, for the Catholic Inquisitors who tortured and burned thousands over a period of several generations, for the depredations of the Conquistadors in the New World, for the European Colonialists and their campaigns to subjugate native populations in Africa and to eradicate them in North and South America, and on and on.

And there is another very conspicuous obstacle to the creation and implementation of a new code of ethics for humanity. This obstacle is a large number of professional people in think tanks, in universities, and in other organizations that have agendas that range from being anti-white, anti-black, anti-Jewish, anti-Islamic, anti-democratic, anti-capitalism, anti-globalism, anti-American, to anti-international business, and more.

As is also obvious, these groups now have the means to reach millions of people daily with their virulent messages. A recent book entitled *Welcome to the Ivory Tower of Babel* by Michael Adams presents a fascinating and frightening portrait of these think-tank and campus-based anti-everything groups.

Guidelines for a New Way of Living

So what might a new social paradigm look like—one that all people could live by and achieve their fullest potential? Given what is known about humanity, the new cultural paradigm would have to include the following elements:

1) That all governments be based on the best principles of democracy [and certainly not the kind of "democracy" that now prevails in the U.S.!]

2) That all societies acknowledge and follow the fundamental principle that females have an equal stake in humanity and must have the same rights and same opportunities as males.

3) That morality be based on dogma-free principles that recognize the true nature of mankind and are designed to nurture all of the elements in the make-up of human beings: the body, the emotions, the intellect and the spirit.

4) That the educational policies of all governments and all educational institutions be redesigned to inculcate all students from day one with a genteel standard of etiquette; a moral value system that includes respect for others, honesty, truthfulness and diligence; a sense of pride in themselves; a sense of honor; the ambition to make the world a better place; and the courage to have big dreams.

5) That the economic policies of all governments be redesigned to further a global-based process of raising the living standards of all people on the planet to a comfortable level.

6) That a key part of this process be providing the means for all females to limit the number of children they have to no more than two.

7) That the finite nature and fragility of Planet Earth be formally and officially recognized and that universal mandatory directives be established to protect and sustain it… balanced with the profit-making that is essential for the well-being of humanity.

8) That these goals be made the basic charter of mankind and be pursued on a global, coordinated basis.

Of course, there are hundreds of other factors, real and imagined, that would have to be a part of this paradigm shift. The goal should be that all societies on the planet become interconnected to the point that they are, in fact, members of a global society. An old idea! A global village!

We are now engaged in three kinds of wars: economic competition; political/military supremacy; and religious ideologies. And that is the new reality of the 21st century. We must therefore strive to bring all countries into the same rational, logical, humane, human family.

Never be bullied into silence.
Never allow yourself to be made a victim.
Accept no one's definition of your life;
define yourself.

—*Harvey Fierstein*—

Much of the world is, in fact, waiting for leaders to create a morality that would lift mankind up and out of the religious, political and economic muck and mire of history.

All of the modern-day institutions have contributed to this moral failure: the political; the business and the educational. All religious institutions have, of course, failed in every facet of their self-proclaimed mandates.

Of course, there is a lot of complaining and wailing about these institutions, particularly education. But most of the institutions are too divided, too hemmed in by laws, too entrenched, and too bureaucratic to reform themselves.

The big hope for humanity is that the new social media that has given voice to the millions of people who know what is good and right and what is bad and wrong, and will join together to browbeat and shame their leaders into making the changes that would allow the human species to achieve much more of its potential, emotionally, intellectually and spiritually.

Fate Facing
Earth and Mankind!

There are more than seven billion human beings on planet Earth and the number is rising by the minute. It is the judgment of experts in many fields that three billion people—less than half of the present number—would be an adequate and sustainable figure.

What is even more telling and frightening is the estimate that at the present rate of growth the number of people on the planet will double within this century if nothing is done to stop it.

By the first decade of the 21st century one half of all of the oxygen-making forests that existed in 1800 had been destroyed; one half of all of the grasslands that existed at that time had also been destroyed. The pace of this destruction is increasing each year to accommodate and feed more people. The race and tribal factors that have fed civil wars and genocide in a number of African countries is one symptom of this competition for land.

To make this image more complete, only some thirty percent of the Earth's surface is land. Of this mass, one-third is covered by sheets of ice around the North and South Poles. Only one-fourth of the ice-free land is even remotely livable—and the melting of the ice sheet around the North Pole will not change this situation.

If the size of population is not controlled it could result in a nightmare scenario that one might see in a horror movie: hundreds of millions or even billions of people living on floating platforms on the Earth's oceans and seas...that have become cesspools of waste.

Pressure from the expanding population is destroying not only forests and grasslands it is also slowly but surely poisoning the oceans, causing the extinction of hundreds to thousands of life forms each year on land and in the seas.

In 2010 the National Research Council of the U.S. released findings revealing that one million tons of carbon dioxide are being absorbed by the world's oceans *every hour of the day*—and that the oceans are now thirty percent more acidic than they were before the Industrial Revolution began in the early 1800s, and that the impact on coral and sea life has already become serious.

The scientists predicted that the acidic content of the oceans will increase by two hundred percent by the end of this century, and even more in the next century if the rate of carbon dioxide production continues to grow.

Human Threat to Animal Life

The primitive id-based urge for human males to kill wild animals, originally for food but now for sport and profit, has already destroyed some of the world's largest animal herds in North America, Africa and Asia. Recently in one area of Africa alone Preserve guards found and confiscated 70,000 traps set for animals by poachers.

Male hunters continue to kill hundreds of thousands of animals each year for sport—in many cases as part of official government programs to keep their numbers down because larger numbers interfere with the lives of people.

In other words, in today's world humans have the right to live and propagate without restraint but animals do not. There is something wrong with that one-sided view of the world.

The religious and economic rationales used to justify the present population growth rate and the destruction of the Earth's plant and animal life are anti-human as well as anti-Earth. This goes beyond being stupid. It is a kind of perverse insanity.

Of course, there are literally millions of people who are aware of this destruction and hundreds of thousands who have been speaking out against it for decades but the system is so large and so powerful their success has been miniscule.

In 2010 the Supreme Court of the United States decreed that the Freedom of Speech provision in the Bill of Rights gives human beings the right to kill, maim and otherwise treat animals cruelly when presented as entertainment. How is that for male-based morality!

The Power of Technology

Since the beginning of the Industrial Revolution in England in the early 1800s the rapid appearance of new technology has done more to change both the behavior and mindset of human beings than anything else since the dawn of human history—and, in fact, is rapidly becoming the new God.

Since the last decades of the 20th century there have been many extraordinary examples of the power of technology to inspire people and change their thinking. These examples have included science fiction movies and television fare—especially *Star Trek*, a preview of the kind of future mankind should and could have.

There are now millions of people who are concerned about the welfare of the planet because of what they have seen and heard in movies and on television, and more and more of them have become active in the growing efforts to protect and present the Earth.

Television has, of course, become the greatest force in making millions of people aware of the threats to the planet—not to mention a new and visceral under-standing of the brutality and horror of war on whatever scale...since it is now visible in all of its blood and gore in the living rooms of people.

On the positive side of present-day TV fare are two documentary films that go beyond the incredible in their revelation of the diversity, the sweep, and the beauty of the Earth and its life forms.

These films include *Planet EARTH*, produced by the British Broadcasting Corporation [BBC]; [with the U.S. version narrated by James Earl Jones, the UK version by Patrick Stewart, the German version by Ulrich Tukur, and the Japanese version by Ken Wata-nabe]; and *Disney's OCEANS*, narrated by Pierce Brosnan.

No one can view these films without being stirred to the depths of their being by the images of the Earth and its life forms, and surely inspired to add their voices to the imperative of protecting and preserving the Earth.

Former U.S. Vice-President Al Gore had already raised the awareness of the fragility of the Earth and the potentially deadly affects of human generated pollution with his film An Inconvenient Truth and in subsequent speeches he made worldwide.

Unfortunately, and in ways that once again empha-sizes both the ignorance and willful stupidity of many people, there was a chorus of criticism aimed at Gore, saying his sources of information about the warming of the Earth were faulty; that he skewered some of his "facts" to reach his conclusions, and that temperatures colder than usual in different parts of the Earth belied his conclusions.

These critics totally ignored indisputable evidence of the melting ice-caps at the north and south poles of the Earth, the rapid disappearance of glaciers all over the world, and the warming of the oceans.

Many of the critics also say that "going green" would result in the disappearance or down-sizing of many industries and have a seriously negative impact on the economies world-wide. It has been repeatedly demonstrated that "going green" would create more jobs than it destroyed.

And it should go without saying that industries that are inherently polluting should be phased out as rapidly as possible.

[17]
Saving
Earth and Humanity!

The common sense of females, the power of technology and a growing number of enlightened males now offer mankind an opportunity to solve what is potentially one of the greatest problems human beings have ever faced—how to get population growth under control and create a new universal cultural paradigm.

Attempts to prevent pregnancy in females go back at least three thousand years [and included some far out methods], but nothing really worked well until the development of the Pill in 1950s by American scientists, and its approval by the Food and Drug Administration in 1960. At that time the typical American woman had 3.6 children—some had as many as a dozen or more...and if Catholic or Mormon, were praised as having been blessed by God.

Just one pill a day was effective over ninety-two percent of the time in preventing pregnancy. Side effects were rare [and have since been virtually eliminated]. When first introduced each pill cost only 12 cents.

At that time, attempts to prevent pregnancy were banned by a number of religions and there were laws in various religious-oriented states and countries making family planning a criminal offense.

By three methods we may learn wisdom:
First, by reflection, which is noblest;
Second, by imitation, which is easiest; and
third by experience, which is the bitterest.

—Confucius—

First, women by the thousands began taking the tiny pill daily despite the laws and religious edicts, and their numbers continued to grow. By 1980 the birth rate among white Americans had dropped below two for the first time in the history of the country.

Despite the fact that the primitive bastions of male power kept up the battle year after year to prevent women from taking the Pill, their numbers soon passed a million, then ten million and by 2010 well over one hundred million.

The gradual unfolding of this pregnancy revolution by American women was chronicled by TIME Magazine in 2010, revealing a battle that started several thousand years ago, and is still in its early stage.

Some of the methods used in an effort to prevent pregnancy in ancient times were bizarre to say the least—including such things as the male putting a ring made from a cut lemon around his penis.

In 1873 the American Congress passed a law labeling birth-control information obscene and banning its distribution to the public—a blatant demonstration of the power of male religious ideologues in Congress.

Well into the 20th century contraception of any kind was opposed by orthodox religions around the world, the most powerful of which even regarded sex within marriage as immoral unless it was aimed at having children. Families with up to fourteen or more children were held up as paragons of moral behavior.

Women who began the push for birth-control methods, including some Catholic women, were treated as criminals. Margaret Sanger, one of the first major figures in this battle, took up the fight after her mother died from complications caused by eighteen pregnancies.

She wrote that she dreamed of a "magic pill." She was arrested and spent time in jail for her efforts.

Not surprisingly, the man who was ultimately responsible for the development of the Pill began his research in an effort to *increase fertility in women who were having trouble conceiving*—not blocking pregnancies!

The emancipation of American women from geting pregnant every twenty-one or twenty-two months was to have a profound influence on the social and economic situation of females, resulting in them swarming into universities and corporate offices by the millions.

By the end of the 20th century some lower level religious leaders had bowed to the inevitable and given grudging approval of the Pill for married women—or they kept quiet about it because they knew large numbers of their members had been using it for many years.

The Political Push Back

Still today there is tremendous opposition to the Pill by critics in some African countries who say it is being used as a political weapon by the White race to limit the number of Blacks—and by dogged God-oriented conservative politicians in the United States who claim the moral high ground by opposing unnatural contraception.

But as history has proven over and over again, nothing changes human behavior faster and more completely than new technology that makes life easier and better. Technology that has benefits that are immediately obvious changes physical behavior virtually instantly—*and a change in thinking inevitably follows.*

Saving the Earth *for* Humanity!

The most important—the most vital—of the steps that must be taken to protect and preserve the Earth and its life forms is to make family planning universal and mandatory on a world-wide basis.

It goes without saying that this is a cultural challenge the likes of which many countries have never faced before. But not meeting the challenge is too horrible to contemplate.

There is, of course, a precedent for this challenge, and that is China, where in 1979 supreme leader Deng Xiaoping decreed that couples in urban Han [racially Chinese] areas of the country could not have more than one child in a desperate measure to stop the ballooning of the population that had already exceeded one billion.

Deng was able to make this draconian policy stick because he had absolute control of the country and did not face the wrath of religious zealots whose God demands that couples have as many children as is physically possible—a practice that traditionally has been more acceptable to men than to women.

In advanced and developing countries the reduction in population growth rate is underway because a growing number of couples are making the decision on their own, regardless of their religious affiliations.

This movement is based on immediate economic factors as well as on a growing awareness that large families are not as desirable as they used to be. But it is far below what is necessary to lower the overall population of the Earth.

Still, it has been shown repeatedly that when wives in poverty-stricken countries are provided with the means to avoid multiple pregnancies many of them will do so.

But achieving a neutral much less negative birth-rate will require a combination of government will on an international basis and a fundamental change in the position of religions that promote large families because it is "God's will."

As said, the world needs some kind of parenting code of ethics that people be taught before they get married and have children—in or outside of wedlock. To start with, courses in parenting responsibilities and skills should be made a mandatory part of the education of the young. But there must be more. There must be a universal family planning program that brings rationality and practicality into procreation.

One of the most critical factors in American society that makes the population problem even more pressing is the preponderance of single women, particular Blacks and Hispanics, who have children—something that has developed because of sexually aggressive and irresponsible males and a government system of supporting single parents.

In earlier times in Catholic Mexico one of the prerogatives of upper class males was to impregnate lower class female employees...a practice also followed by owners of black slaves in early America.

The political, economic and social policies of promoting growth and more growth for the sake of profit and power must be eliminated from the human mindset. Economic growth should first of all be designed to raise the level of the living standard of all people on Earth to a comfortable level that it is sustainable.

The battle for women's right to control the number of children they have is far from over. Individual religious zealots in the private sector as well as many who are in public office are keeping the fight going by opposing family planning in any form or fashion—with many resorting to mental and physical intimidation and some to murder.

National polls show that over two-thirds of young American males and females believe that the ability to prevent unwanted pregnancies is important, but sixty-three percent say they know very little about birth control pills, and much of what they say they know is wrong.

All public institutions and organizations, including the religions, should join together to make the Pill available to females worldwide. Each Pill costs only a few cents to produce, and they could be made available for free-pickup in places in every city, town, village and rural area in the world.

But the responsibility of controlling the population of the Earth should not and will not be left up to females alone. Dramatic advances had been made by scientists in the development of new means of preventing conception that are designed for men.

Whether or not males make use of this new technology will be the ultimate test of their concern, both for their female partners and the Earth.

The Population-Growth Sickness!

In the past, the proselytizing success that Christianity has had has invariably been in poor countries where women especially were oppressed. These successes did not come from the theology or spirituality the missionaries preached but from the gender and social reforms that were inherent or added in their message.

The mistreated and unhappy people in these countries should have learned long ago that believing in, bowing before, and praying to spirits and gods did not improve their political or social situation one iota. That was something that required fundamental reforms in political and social institutions over which they had no control whatsoever.

The Mormon religion is one partial exception in the proselytizing gambit to increase its membership. Notwithstanding the infantile fable of its founding, the Mormon Church follows a system that in many respects is far more practical and positive than that of competing religions.

Its emphasis on language and culture learning, on strict dress and behavior and on business acumen has made it a powerful force that attracts and holds people born into Mormon families. The method of child-upbringing designed by male members of the Mormon Church incorporates brainwashing techniques, and it works.

But the positive side of the Mormon campaign to increase its number of members does not alter the fact that the whole population-growth concept is like a virus that has infected the Big Three religions since their founding.

The religious-economic-political concept that prosperity and the quality of life is based on a continuously growing population is not only out-dated, it is one of the primary factors in the poverty that plagues over half of the population of the Earth, including millions of people in the most prosperous nations. It is also one of the primary sources of much of the violence that afflicts so much of mankind.

The Economic Growth Obsession

Another vital factor in saving the Earth is eliminating the political, economic and social policies of promoting economic growth and more growth for the sake of profit and power. Economic growth should first of all be designed to raise the level of the living standard of all people on Earth to a comfortable level that it is sustainable—and then economic policies should be based on improving the quality of life.

This is another area that must be addressed by not only by the education system but by the news media, the business world, the political establishments, and by ordinary people who understand that there must be a limit to economic growth.

The Gross National Product [GNP] of a nation should not be the standard by which it is measured. That is a mindset that inevitably leads to irrational and immoral behavior. It permeates a culture and leads to competition that in turn can and has led to war.

There are some societies that are not as obsessed with GNP as the United States, China, Japan and other industrialized nations. But to my knowledge as of this writing only tiny Bhutan in Southeast Asia has an official policy that promotes *Gross National Happiness* [GNH] instead of GNP. There were, however, a growing number of countries that were beginning to give more priority to GNH, including [not surprisingly] France, resulting in many foreigners beating up on the French for their "irrational" behavior.

Transforming a society from an economic base to a happiness base is an educational challenge. It will not happen from the top down. It must be a personal choice made by individuals and families and grow from the bottom up.

More on the Problem of Sex

Throughout history most human beings have desired only to live in peace and be safe and secure, but they have not had the power to dispute or ignore their religious and political rulers who added to rather than solved the problem of human sexuality.

The misunderstanding and abuse of human sexuality is not going to go away until we manage to create a new ethic for sexual behavior that is rational, satisfying and doable.

Just one of thousands of daily examples of the inadequacies of the present system: in India official statistics estimate that there are some 1.2 million child prostitutes. The number of child prostitutes in African nations and in other nations as well, including the United States, is both staggering and astonishing.

There is no mystery at all as to why this incredible situation exists and has existed for millennia. In short, the sexual nature of the human male, male-dominated religions and male-dominated political, economic and social systems are responsible.

This situation will not be eradicated until enough men of goodwill find the courage and the voice to defy the misplaced moral teachings of religions and other anti-human ideologists to demand that the sexual nature of human beings be recognized and a rational, practical system for accommodating this nature be accepted as the norm.

Interestingly, as is almost always the case when it comes to cultural changes, it will be younger people, not leaders, who bring the final solution to the sex problem—and with the entertainment and news industries now pushing the process and the Internet providing them with instant access to billions of people that could happen within the 21st century.

When this happens the sex-based advertising, entertainment and news-based industries as well as the anti-sex positions of religions will have to find something else to justify their existence. With the time span of each generation getting shorter and shorter, there may yet be foreseeable hope for humanity.

A Willful Stupidity Checklist

While it is true that in recent decades human beings have accomplished things that are god-like, we have not only continued to behave with willful stupidity, we have dramatically enlarged on the variety and volume of stupid things we do—knowing that they are harmful to people, to all other life forms, and to the planet.

The following things can be ranked among the most stupid and most damaging characteristics of humans—all of which impact on the motivation and ability of parents and teachers to educate the young.

1] The widespread existence of violence in every form imaginable, from mental and physical abuse to murder and war—most often committed by men.

2] Belief in male-created religious dogma that re-presses natural human behavior—especially our gene-tically programmed sexuality—and encourages dis-crimination and violence against non-believers—the latter invariably perpetrated by men.

3] The male-led adoption of the profit motive as the primary human morality, overriding all of the valid moral teachings of religions and philosophers.

4] The creation of huge entertainment industries based on appealing to unfulfilled sexual appetites that reli-gions have traditionally sought to repress, thus creating the market.

5] The display of female sexuality as a come-on to attract attention to products and services because fe-male sexuality has been denied, covered up, abused and limited by religious-based social customs and laws, creating an obsessive interest in it.

6] Built-in male discrimination against different races, colors and religious creeds caused by ego-based self-interest, tribalism, territorialism and the thirst for pow-er and control.

7] The glorification of the use of drugs by the enter-tainment industries and the concentrated efforts of the medicinal drug industry to get more people to take more drugs in a profit-making conspiracy with the medical field.

8] The breakdown of the male-female family unit as the primary structure of societies, and the growing number of males who impregnate single females and take no role in the upbringing of the children they sire.

9] The failure of more and more parents in indust-rialized countries to take responsibility for civilizing and educating their children, leaving it up to television, video games and "conveyor-belt" schools.

10] The reality that virtually all of the organized struc-tures of modern society—business, education, govern-ment, health—are primarily based on self-interest within a mish-mash of guidelines and rules that are self-limiting if not self-defeating.

Virtually all of these failings—and more—are the result of willful stupidity, and that is not going to go away or be significantly reduced until we have a uni-versal cultural paradigm based on a rational philoso-phy in place and working.

The Need for a Universal Philosophy

Again, it goes without saying that god-based religions have never succeeded in ensuring a rational and con-structive standard of human behavior. Far too many of their concepts and dogmas simply did not fit the human condition even when most people had little understanding or little learning beyond the basics of staying alive and continuing the species.

As said, the teaching and belief that there is a divine Creator who watches over and protects people, accepts their souls into Heaven when they die or sends them to Hell if they have broken any rules and don't accept Jesus Christ as their Savior before dying is primitive nonsense and the ultimate cop-out!*

---

*To read an extraordinarily detailed account of the Biblical myths, exaggerations and lies about the birth, life and death of the young Jewish male who well after his execution became known as Jesus Christ, see the book, *Born of a Woman,* by noted bishop and religious scholar John Shelby Spong.

After the death of Isa [Jesus] his followers began referring to him as Eashoa [or Yeshua] Msheekhah in Aramiac, the language of his birth. That is now translated into English as Christ the Anointed One—the word Christ coming from the Greek term khristos [christos], which means "oil." But in the mindset of Christians it equates with the Son of God.

Spong's book, copiously annotated with exact quotes from the Bible, clearly reveals that the Biblical claims of the divinity of Jesus and his "miracles" are simply stories written from decades to hundreds of years later that were designed to influence ignorant people to believe that Isa did not have a biological father, despite having been born to Mary, a very human female, and was the Son of God manifested in human flesh.

Even more interesting, Spong details Biblical accounts which suggest that the reason for these stories about the birth of Isa was to cover up the fact that he was an illegitimate child. The claimed divinity of Isa did not become an article of Christian faith until long after he was executed with the willing help of his Jewish competitors who resented his popularity among the poor and oppressed. He was no doubt a great teacher who attracted followers because he taught love instead of hate;

generosity instead of greed; cooperation instead of conflict—all of which were rampant in his time.

One of the great mysteries about the Biblical Jesus was where he was and what he was doing from the age of 12—when the Bible first mentions him—and the age of 33 or 34, when he showed up at the Jordan River, was baptized by John the Baptist and began a ministry that lasted for only two to three years.

There is an astounding legend in Japan—supported by documentary evidence—that Jesus and his brother Isukiri spent many of these missing years in Japan in a village called Herai [later renamed Shingō], that he and his brother returned to Jordan when he was 33 or 34 but that it was Isukiri who was crucified by the Romans, not Jesus. The legend goes on to say that Jesus returned to Herai, married a Japanese woman, became a rice farmer, had children, and died there of old age. His tomb, and an adjoining tomb for his brother, can still be seen in Herai.

It is the position of the Jewish and Christian faiths that God and Jesus Christ are the only true sources of the wisdom that human beings must have to live decent, upright lives—a position obviously taken by the creators of these religions because they had no source for enlightened intelligence beyond common sense.

The rules regarding charity, goodwill, honesty and other common sense things that these spiritual leaders prescribed obviously represented the ideal behavior for all human beings so the God they created naturally appealed to people, and attracted followers.

The trouble is fear of a vengeful God and the threat of spending eternity in Hell were not powerful enough to make all men obey these simple dictates, resulting in Jewish and Christian leaders taking enforcement into their own hands, using a variety of cruel methods to punish both nonbelievers and turncoats.

In earlier times this historical dichotomy in Judaism, Christianity and Islam did not reduce their power over people, but with the spread of education in modern times the religions have lost much of their relevance for a large percentage of people.

And yet, the ideal human traits promoted by all of the religions are still very much alive and well among most people, with an astounding level of goodwill and charity when it comes to helping those in need.

However, it should also be obvious by this time that the God of Judaism and Christianity and the God of Islam do not watch over or take care of anyone. And it certainly doesn't do any good to credit "Him" for success and good luck, or to blame Him for all of the tragedies that befall mankind on a daily basis. All of these things are a result of nature doing its thing combined with the bad freewill of individuals.

Human beings cannot become truly rational, sane and civilized until they stop depending on mythical gods and all other irrational elements of cultures, and accept full responsibility for their thoughts and actions.

Again, the answer to the question and the dilemma of human behavior is not religion. It is a universal philosophy based on a simple, rational set of rules that are culturally neutral and apply to everyone.

And here the valid principles of the above religions would come into play—goodwill, no lying, no stealing, no killing, cooperation, taking care of the planet, and so on—with individuals taking personal responsibility for their behavior.

On the "human-beings-as-god" front, well before the end of the first half of this century people will be able to get their DNA sequenced and will have a map of what it means to be human and what the future may hold for them health and longevity wise.

By the end of this century sequencing the genomes of all common life forms will be routine, providing road maps for altering and or improving them.

The sequencing of the genomes of all diseases will make it possible create remedies for them and eventually eliminate them altogether. The sequencing of matter is already well underway and is resulting in new materials never before seen or even imagined that will impact life on virtually every level.

Advances in all areas of science are becoming a daily thing—advances that will continue to transform what people do and how they do it.

The day of man as the real god-creator is at hand, but the question remains: can mankind ever be a benevolent god?

The Make-Up of Human Beings

There are four elements in the make-up of human beings: the physical, the emotional, the intellectual and the spiritual. None of these elements have any connection or relationship whatsoever with an outside divine force, but they do have an inseparable relationship with nature and the cosmos at large.

The Physical Element

The first of these elements that must be understood and dealt with is the physical. In simple terms, this refers to the feeding and care of infants and children as they grow up and mature; needs that adults are expected to provide.

If there are weaknesses or incomplete factors in the care of the physical needs of infants and children the emotional element in their make-up will be affected to varying degrees, depending on the seriousness of the actions or non-actions that affect them.

It is during the first five or six years of the life of individuals that they are normally civilized—that is taught to behave in what is regarded as a proper or acceptable manner—and this is a responsibility that normally falls to parents or other adults.

Wise men and women learned a long time ago that when good behavior—and knowledge—are taught as physical subjects, not just as mental exercises, they become embedded in the body and mind and have a lasting effect.

"Body memory," as all great athletes, artists and performers know, is far more powerful and important than mental memory. Imagine master piano players having to consciously remember the locations of all of the keys they have to hit and in what order and consciously direct their fingers to each individual key as they play.

Both positive attitudes and civilized social behavior can and should be instilled into the mind-body of individuals to the point that they become automatic by the time they reach the age of six or seven.

The Emotional Element

The emotional element in the make-up of human beings is based on several factors: the emotional gene-based make-up of the individual at birth; the sex of the individual; the character and personality of the parents or parent and other older individuals who interact with them; the overall home environment; the kind and quality of education they receive, and a host of other big and little things that influence the mindset of infants and small children.

In other words, the character and quality of the emotional element of each individual is determined by a variety of factors, many of which cannot be changed while others are subject to change but are more or less based on circumstances.

The Intellectual Element

The intellect refers to the higher order of the mind that understands things, that makes choices and decisions based on rational, logical thinking and whatever experience and knowledge an individual has accumulated.

The control of the intellect comes under the heading of philosophy, which refers to the love and pursuit of wisdom and moral self-discipline, with moral self-discipline being the key factor.

Unfortunately, Americans have traditionally viewed philosophy as the province of eggheads who just sit around and think; not as one of the most essential elements of civilization and daily life.

Without a rational and humane philosophy of life there are no dependable compasses or guidelines for behavior, which is the reason why so many well-educated and experienced people do such terrible things.

It is obvious that the present-day child-raising and the educational systems in the U.S. and elsewhere do not get passing grades in either of these two areas.

The intellectual capacity of children is partially fixed at birth, and is apparently a genetic thing. Some children are simply born with a higher intellect than others, are more curious, and learn faster than others.

In rare cases some children display genius attributes by the time they are two years old—or even younger—without any input by parents or other adults. If recognized and encouraged, some of these children become great inventors, mathematicians, musicians and so on.

It has been shown that all children except those whose brains are deficient at birth can learn much faster and far more complicated facts and concepts at a younger age than most parents are aware of or do anything about. This adult/parental failure is a cultural-educational thing first and often an economic thing second.

The key factor in the intellectual character and capacity of individuals as they grow up is determined by the kind and quality of the informal and formal education they are exposed to; which in turn is determined by the living standard, lifestyle, education and mindset of their parents and the overall culture of their society.

At this time, the intellectual level of large number of Americans is probably the lowest among the more advanced countries of the world.

The Spiritual Element

One of the most critical factors in the make-up of human beings is the spiritual element...and this does not refer to a belief in some god-based religious dogma, which is often so far removed from reality that it is both ludicrous and anti-human.

It refers instead to the relationship that all human beings have with all other living creatures and material things, from rocks and trees to water and to the cosmos at large.

Scientists have shown that all of the material elements making up the universe, including the bodies of all living things, were created by hydrogen-fueled exploding stars. We are therefore children of the stars or the cosmos at large, if you prefer the big picture. Nature is the great Creator. It creates and destroys in an inexorable rhythm that has been going on for billions of years and will apparently continue for many more billions. Human beings are late-comers in the trial-and-error methods of the cosmos, and claim to be the most intelligent species of life so far.

It is clear that the solution to the spiritual element in human affairs will not be found in any organized religion, but in personal actions taken by individuals, based on nurturing and strengthening our relationships with all of nature and the universe.

This effort does not entail anything supernatural, divine or religious in any sense. You might define it as a manifestation of the "force" that brings life to the body and mind. This spirit or life-force is something like a battery that runs our bodily functions, our thinking and most of our physical actions.

The power of this life-force, which various greatly in individuals, can be increased by exercises that challenge both the body and the mind. It can also be increased by learning how to focus the mind on a single thing—or emptying the mind altogether.

When the "spirit battery" is fully charged and working properly it includes such elements as courage, determination, diligence regarding both large and small things, perseverance in pursuing goals, an appreciation for form and order, harmonious personal relationships, and respect for all things.

The Distant Dream

All of the prevailing reasons why men go to war—religion, the hunger for political power, the obsession with wealth, territorial ambitions, oppressive government regimes—should be eliminated by a coordinated universal effort that now seems to be so far beyond the ability of mankind that it is not even a dream. But that is exactly what at least ninety-five percent of the people on Earth want! So why can't it be done?

It *can* be done but it will not be done until religious and political leaders are no longer in the dark ages where ignorance, irrationality and inhuman behavior are the norm—the norm for them; not for the people at large—or until new more powerful forces transform the mindset of humanity...a phenomenon that is already underway.

It is obvious that the material quality of life is primarily determined by knowing what to do and having the political and religious freedom to do it. This makes it imperative that all people be freed from the destructive religious, political and economic shackles of the past.

It is also imperative that the excess-consumption syndrome be eliminated from the world's economic systems, and that people be encouraged and helped to create life-styles that are physically, emotionally, spiritually and intellectually satisfying that are not based on excess material things.

Ordinary people have to become revolutionaries, willing to resist and to fight the status quo, and force all of the established power centers to do what is common sense and morally right for humanity and the Earth.

But still the Earth needs great leaders who are selfless and unrelenting in their efforts to protect and preserve the planet and mankind. As the great Chinese sage Lao Tzu said ages ago: "A great leader has no self-interest and leaves no trace. When he is finished the people say, 'We did it ourselves.'"

Lao also said that the more laws you have the more laws will be broken; and "When taxes are too high, people go hungry. When the government is too intrusive, people lose their spirit."

The basic solution to the negative and destructive influence of male dominance and religious nonsense is fact-based gender-equal education.

The New Education Paradigm

It had become more than obvious by the end of the 20th century that the American system of education was still stuck in the 1800s—that it was not educating children for the present challenges and that the decline in the economic, political and social fortunes of the United States could be traced in large part to failures in education.

Most people were not blind to this failing but the built-in bureaucracy and mindset of the bureaucrats and politicians in charge of the system made it impossible to reform the education process in fundamental ways.

However, on the fringes of the huge system there were efforts by many to bring both the process and content of education up-to-date. One of the most successful of these efforts was the Kahn Academy, a non-profit organization created in 2006 by Salman Kahn, a Bangladeshi-American graduate of the Massachusetts Institute of Technology who decided on his own to provide both students and teachers with an alternative to the failed system that was still based on methods and subjects that were over a hundred years old.

Kahn's website-based system provides over 2,600 video tutorials stored on YouTube and available free of charge to teachers and students. The lectures and illustrations on the videos cover mathematics, history, finance, physics, chemistry, biology, astronomy, economics and computer science.

The tutorials encourage students who are faster learners than others to act as personal tutors to their own classmates...something that makes the classrooms lively places that resemble game rooms where the game is learning.

The system takes into account that all students are different; that they have different learning capabilities and different personalities, and learn at different speeds. It also benefits from the fact that kids learn faster from interacting with other kids than they do listening to teachers lecture and reading books that are not interactive.

In other words, the system of teaching is personalized and customized for individual students—something the traditional system has not and cannot do.

By the end of the first decade of the 21st century it was already obvious that technology was reshaping the model of education; that little by little teaching in most categories was transitioning into facilitating the use of technology—much of it in the hands of students themselves.

This is already having a fundamental impact not only on how students learn but what they learn because they are no longer chained to the institutionalized and ritualized methods and sources of learning. The future of both old, traditional teaching materials and teaching styles will hopefully be short, and this could be one of the fastest cultural transitions in the history of mankind.

This transition in teaching and learning can help lead to the reforming of all elements of the cultures of the world if it is allowed and encouraged to continue.

How wonderful it is
that nobody need wait
a single moment
before starting
to improve the world!

—Anne Frank—

(Teenage Jewish girl killed by the Nazis during
World War II, after she was hidden in an attic for several
years during which she kept a diary that has since become
a perennial bestseller)